Walter Davis Dabney

The Public Regulation of Railways

Walter Davis Dabney

The Public Regulation of Railways

ISBN/EAN: 9783337784331

Printed in Europe, USA, Canada, Australia, Japan

Cover: Foto ©Andreas Hilbeck / pixelio.de

More available books at **www.hansebooks.com**

The Public Regulation
of Railways

BY

W. D. DABNEY

FORMERLY CHAIRMAN OF THE COMMITTEE ON RAILWAYS AND INTERNAL
NAVIGATION IN THE LEGISLATURE OF VIRGINIA

NEW YORK & LONDON
G. P. PUTNAM'S SONS
The Knickerbocker Press
1889

CONTENTS.

                                                                                             PAGE

PUBLIC REGULATION OF RAILWAYS: *Its Legal and Economic Aspects Briefly Considered* 1–5

    CHAPTER I.—*The Legal Aspects of the Question* . 5–26

Sources of Legislative Power.—The Railroad a Public Highway.—Eminent Domain and Taxation in Aid of its Construction.—General Competition over Railroads.—Interchange of Traffic.—Public Character of Uses to Which Railroad Property is Dedicated.—Mode of Use and Price of Use Matters of Legislative Regulation, unless Restricted by Charter Contracts.—Delegation of Power.

    CHAPTER II. 27–44

Limitation on Legislative Power Arising from Charter Contracts.—Strictly Construed against the Corporations.—Not Binding Where Power to Amend, Alter, or Repeal Charters is Reserved to the Legislature.—Examples of Application of the Power to Amend, Alter, or Repeal.—Dual Character of Railroad Property Considered.—Private Ownership Restricted to Public Use.—Right of Public Use Paramount to Private Ownership.

    CHAPTER III. 45–65

Limitation on Legislative Power Arising from the Private Property Rights of Owners of Railways or Railway Securities.—Power to Regulate Railway Charges, Analogous to Power of Eminent Domain.—Can Only be Exercised for the Accomplishment of Some Public Good, and must Not Deprive Owners of Reasonable Income on Just Value of Property.—Just Value Distinguished from Capitalization.—Regulation not Equivalent to Confiscation.—Distinction between Charges Fixed by Public Authority for Specific Services, and the Entire Schedule of Rates as a Whole.—The Latter Ultimately Subject to Judicial Revision.—The Tilley Case (U. S. Circuit Court in Georgia) and Cases from Supreme Court Compared.—Recent Iowa Cases.

CHAPTER IV. 66–88

Limitation on State Powers Arising from Exclusive Right of Congress to "Regulate Commerce among the States."—Interstate Commerce Defined and Illustrated.—States cannot Regulate Charges Thereon, and Probably cannot Prevent Traffic Arrangements between Its Own and Foreign Corporations in Respect Thereto.—But Leases and Consolidations between Domestic and Foreign Corporations Probably under Control of States and not of Congress.—Sources and Limitations of Powers of Congress Discussed.

CHAPTER V.—*The Economic Aspects of the Question* 89–131

Extortion.—Discriminations of Various Kinds.—Relations of Railroads to Each Other and to Water Routes.—Results thereof.—Competition and Monopoly.—Relative Charges for Long and Short Distances.—Illustrations and Effects Thereof. Discussion of the Long- and Short-Haul Question.—Under What Circumstances and Conditions a Greater Charge for a Shorter Haul Justifiable.—Illustrations and Analogies.

CHAPTER VI. 132–174

Personal Discriminations.—Resulting from Excessive Competition; from Supposed Advantages to Accrue to the Railroads Therefrom; from Mere Favoritism.—Never Justifiable.—Distinguished from Local Discriminations.—Difficulty of Detection.—The Pooling System.—Differential Rates.—Unnecessary Railroad Building.—Division of Territory.—Consolidations.—Discrimination between Different Kinds of Traffic, or Classification of Freight.—Value and Risk, and Not Cost of Service, the Basis of Classification.—Necessity to the Public Welfare of the Adoption of this Basis.—Abuses.

PAGE

CHAPTER VII. 175–205

Methods Adopted or Proposed to Prevent Extortion and Unjust Discrimination.—Publication of Rates.—Statistical Reports.—English "Railway and Canal Traffic Act."—Remedial Statutes Usually of Little Avail.—The Commission System.—Power to Fix Rates ; to Revise Rates ; to Hear and Decide Complaints ; to Hear Complaints and Make Recommendations. — Examples. — Georgia and Massachusetts.—Theory of General Unrestricted Competition over the Same Line of Road Reviewed.—Destructive of Commerce in Many Necessities of Life.—Monopoly Essential to Public Interest.—Theory of Public Ownership Reviewed.—Would Fail to Prevent Discriminations.

CHAPTER VIII.—*The Interstate Commerce Act* . 206–261

Analysis of the Act.—Powers of Commission.—Decisions concerning Long and Short Haul.—Discriminations between Places, Persons, and Kinds of Traffic.—Effects of the Act.—Tendency toward Combination.—A Railway " Trust."

CHAPTER IX.—*Express Traffic* . . . 262–281

The Relations of Express to Railroad Carriers one of Contract Merely.—Effect of Wars of Express Rates on Railway Charges and Earnings.—The Express Company the Means of Warfare between Rival Railroads.—The Case of the Express Companies before Congress and the Commission.

PUBLIC REGULATION OF RAILWAYS:

ITS LEGAL AND ECONOMIC ASPECTS BRIEFLY CONSIDERED.

HAVING occupied the position of chairman of a legislative committee, entrusted with the preparation of legislation upon this subject, I was unable to find in convenient and accessible form a discussion of many of the difficulties which surround it.

Among a number of works examined, that of Professor Hadley entitled " Railroad Transportation " was found the most interesting and valuable. But even this—admirable as the treatise is—responds either inadequately or not at all to many inquiries which arise in the attempt to formulate legislation. In the four years which have elapsed since the publication of Mr. Hadley's work, much new light has been thrown upon the general question, and with its aid I have attempted in the following pages to make some suggestions of a practical character, upon a subject whose intricacies can only be appreciated by one who has attempted their solution.

The title which, for want of a better, has been prefixed to this essay may, however, imply an undertaking which is far beyond its scope. It is proper therefore to say that it proposes to deal only with the *commercial* or *traffic relations* of the railway system to the public, and contemplates no discussion of those *police powers* and regulations which pertain to the physical condition of railroads, and their operation with reference to public safety and convenience. It is intended to be suggestive only, not exhaustive. Its object is merely: 1st, to point out in as plain and popular a manner as possible a few principles which have been authoritatively laid down, defining or suggesting the sources and the limitations of legislative power in this country over railroads and railroad transportation; and 2d, to discuss briefly the chief causes of complaint against railway practices in the United States, and the methods, policy, and propriety of public regulation of commerce by railways.

On the subject of legislative authority, the decisions of the United States Supreme Court will be appealed to, almost exclusively—that tribunal having the ultimate determination of nearly all questions of that character. One or two important cases in the lower Federal courts will, however, also be commented upon, and a few in the higher State courts will be referred to.

The discussion of the economic aspects of the question will be based principally upon material contained in the reports and decisions of the Interstate Commerce Commission, and in the testimony and arguments adduced before that body; in reports of various State Railroad Commissions, reports of the National Bureau of Statistics, reports of investigating committees of legislative bodies, and the testimony taken by them, and especially upon the report made and the testimony taken by the select committee of the United States Senate, commonly called the "Cullom Committee."

References to authorities will usually be specifically given, but in the course of inquiries into this subject, in which as a member of a legislative body I have taken part, much valuable information has been given me which I can only acknowledge in a general way. Certain facts and principles apparently well established will be commented on to illustrate the necessity for some public supervision over the railroad system, and certain circumstances and conditions of railroad transportation will be discussed and illustrated, which make some of the most popular legislative enactments upon this subject of very doubtful propriety and probably harmful results.

A brief analysis will be given of the law of Congress commonly called the "Interstate Commerce Act," and a short *résumé* of a few of the principal rulings and decisions of the commission under that act, to illustrate its practical operation.

The vast and growing importance of the express business in the commerce of the country, and its intimate connection with the railway transportation system, calls for some discussion of the relations between carriers by express and ordinary carriers by rail, in the discharge of their public functions. Accordingly a chapter will be devoted to that subject.

W. D. DABNEY.

CHARLOTTESVILLE, Va.
July, 1889.

THE LEGAL ASPECTS OF THE QUESTION.

CHAPTER I.

Sources of Legislative Power—The Railroad a Public Highway—Eminent Domain and Taxation in Aid of its Construction—General Competition over Railroads—Interchange of Traffic—Public Character of Uses to which Railroad Property is Dedicated—Mode of Use and Price of Use Matters of Legislative Regulation, unless Restricted by Charter Contracts—Delegation of Power.

IT has been said concerning the construction of the political constitution of the country, that nothing is so important as a frequent recurrence to first principles. The same remark is applicable to a correct understanding of the relations of the railway system to the public.

There can be no doubt that the system as it has developed, and as it it is now operated, has drifted far away from the principles on which it derived its existence, and to understand fully the right and the extent of public control over the system, an examination of those principles is necessary. The notion upon which railroads came into being, and upon which many early charters were drawn, was that any and all persons might have the use of the road, for the transit of their own vehicles by their own motive power, upon the payment of reasonable "tolls" to the owners of the road. The common use of this word "tolls" in respect to railroad charges indicates the prevalent idea entertained as to the character of which railroad transportation would partake—namely, that of the turnpike. And the word is still in frequent use, though as a general thing its original signification no longer applies in this connection.

The modern function of the railroad company as the exclusive carrier upon its own road has become so familiar, that it is somewhat difficult to realize fully the original conception of its function, as a highway upon which numerous carriers might compete for business.

But there is no necessary connection between the two functions of furnishing the road, and carrying upon it. Much less is there any legal reason why the railroad company should be the exclusive carrier over its road. Its right to carry at all, and more especially its exclusive right, depends upon the terms of its charter. This historical view, with the legal relations resulting from it, are clearly recognized in the jurisprudence of the subject. The Supreme Court of the United States has examined the question in this light,[1] and the fair inference from the remarks of the Court is, that in the absence of provision to the contrary, the railway is, theoretically at least, a public

---

[1] L., S., & M. Railroad Co. *vs.* United States. 93 U. S., p. 442.

highway, and as such open for the transit of the vehicles of all persons, upon payment of reasonable tolls, and subject to reasonable regulations.

It is undoubtedly true that "in practice, as a general thing, railroads are only operated by companies that own them, or by those with whom they have permanent arrangements for the purpose. The companies have a practical if not a legal monopoly of their use." But "the ascertained impracticability of the general and indiscriminate use of these great thoroughfares, does not preclude their use by transportation companies having no interest in the roads themselves." The general course of legislation "sufficiently demonstrates the fact, that in the early history of railroads it was quite generally supposed that they could be public highways in fact, as well as in name."

And "this fact affords the only explanation of much of the language used, not only in those early charters, but in many of those which have been granted since, the latter adopting, as was natural, the forms of phraseology found prepared to hand." It has also been judicially declared,[1] that the exercise of the right of eminent domain, in the construction of railroads, and the levy of taxes to raise subsidies in their aid, are justified only by the fact that railroads are public highways. "That railroads though constructed by private corporations and owned by them are public highways, has been the doctrine of nearly all the courts ever since such conveniences for passage and trans-

---

[1] Olcott *vs.* The Supervisors, 16 Wall, 678.

portation have had any existence." "It has never been considered a matter of any importance that the road was built by the agency of a private corporation. No matter who is the agent, the function performed is that of the State. Though the ownership is private the use is public." "It is said that railroads are not public highways *per se ;* that they are only declared such by the decisions of the courts." "This is a mistake; in their very nature they are public highways. It needed no decision of the courts to make them such." " As well might it be said a turnpike is a highway only because declared such by judicial decision." "That all persons may not put their own cars upon the road, and use their own motive power, has no bearing upon the question whether the road is a public highway. It bears only upon the mode of use, of which the legislature is the exclusive judge."

This assertion of the power of the legislature over the mode of use of railways, that is, whether the right of transportation over a railroad shall be exclusively in the company which owns it, or whether it shall be open to all comers, upon payment of tolls (and under proper regulations), is one, as will subsequently appear, of great practical importance. The unrestricted application to the present railroad system, of the original idea of free competition, would no doubt present very grave difficulties and physical danger in the operation of railways; and would, moreover, as will be shown in another connection, paralyze the transportation business as applied to many of the most necessary articles of commerce and of civilized existence. But for these difficulties, the application upon any railroad line of the theory of free competition, might, in some branches of trade and transportation, be highly beneficial, and might result in a partial solution, at least, of many of the most perplexing problems of railroad transportation. However unwise might be the exercise of the power to open railways to general competition, it can hardly be doubted that, in the absence of contract restrictions, the legislature possesses that power, —taking care, of course, to secure to the owners of the roads reasonable compensation for their use. The question of legislative power thus broadly suggested is hardly a practical one, but it may become of great importance when sought to be applied to compel railway companies to permit the unrestricted "interchange of traffic" over their respective roads, which may frequently be of consequence to the public welfare. Many modern charters and the general railroad laws of some States provide, however, that "the company shall have the exclusive right of transportation over its own road." This language was doubtless used to exclude the well settled idea— drawn from the analogy of the public road or turnpike— that the ownership of the railroad would be vested in one set of persons, and the vehicles of transportation upon it —the cars or "carriages"—would belong to others. The language probably amounts to a *contract* between the public and the railroad company, conferring an exclusive privilege, which would not otherwise belong to the latter, and of which (if the legislature can validly make such a contract) the company cannot be deprived by future legislative act, unless the right to amend, alter, and repeal charters has been reserved.

The word "*transportation*" suggests two things, namely, motive power, and vehicles for carriage. The language that "the company shall have the exclusive right of transportation over its road," therefore conveys the idea that its own motive power and its own vehicles shall both, exclusively of all others, be used. And to compel the company to haul the vehicles of others, with its own motive power, would be as much an infringement of the right that language confers, as to compel it to allow others to have the use of its track for their engines and cars.

It has been questioned by some writers,[1] whether a legislature can confer, by contract with a railroad company, an exclusive right to the use of its road. This, it is said, has the appearance of a perversion of the road to the private use of its owners; and the power of eminent domain, as has been seen, can only be conferred by the legislature for a public use. So that to grant to a railroad company the prerogative right of eminent domain, and then grant the right to use it for private, in subordination to public ends, would be to endow the company with inconsistent privileges, one or the other of which must be

---

[1] See "The Railways and the Republic," by J. F. Hudson.

void. If the former be void, the company has no title to its road, if the latter be void, the public right of use has not been impaired by the legislation. Such is the argument against the legislative power to confer the exclusive right of transportation over a railroad, upon a single corporation. It assumes that the exclusive use is necessarily the perversion of the road from public to private objects. But if the public object be—as it undoubtedly is—the general good of the whole community, this assumption is erroneous. That object, it is believed, has been best secured, and will be best maintained, by giving to every company the exclusive right of carrying over its own line, subject to the duty of such free interchange of traffic with connecting roads as the public good may require. And this "is a matter of which the legislature is the exclusive judge."

This question becomes a practical one, when one railroad company seeks to secure with a connecting road an arrangement for mutual interchange of traffic, which the latter refuses to enter into. Such an arrangement would involve the free and unrestricted passage of the cars of one company over the roads of the other—subject, of course, to reasonable inspection and regulations, for safety and convenience.

These arrangements—now almost universal among railroad companies—do not involve the payment of *tolls* by one company to the other, for the use of its track. Each road furnishes its own motive power, and its own train men. It charges for the services both of furnishing the road and of carrying upon it, and it pays the connecting road, in whose cars the traffic is received and carried, a fixed sum per mile for the use of its cars. This arrangement shows how completely the idea of "tolls" (in the original signification of the word) is eliminated from modern railroad practice. Still the right to have the vehicles of one company pass over the road of another is necessarily involved, and raises the question of legislative power to declare and enforce such a right.

In the actual exigencies of business, however, the question is presented, not alone, but in association with others. These other questions are as to issuing joint through bills of lading, and through tickets over connecting roads, so that both may be used by the public as a continuous and uninterrupted means of communication; joint use of terminal facilities at points of junction; the proportion of the joint through rate over the connecting roads, that each one shall receive; the price to be paid by each for the use of the other's cars; and in general all the arrangements necessary and proper for the "through" carriage of passengers and freight over connecting lines.

Upon the subject of the rights and interest of the public in railway connections, and in the free interchange of traffic between connecting or intersecting lines, a quotation is here inserted from Col. T. H. Carter, once railroad commissioner of Virginia, and now chief commissioner of the Southern Railway and Steamship Association. "It is," said he, " surely incumbent on the connecting lines under the law, and under every consideration of equity, to afford every facility rather than to offer the slightest obstruction to the free flow of trade and travel. . . . They have no right to refuse rates in one direction, which they recognize under similar circumstances in another, simply because it is to their own interests to do so. They have no right to refuse full and free access to and from other roads, simply because by so controlling the current of trade and travel, they secure to themselves perforce, a larger proportion of it. They have no right either to refuse to connect with other roads, or to so regulate their connections, as to break in upon the continuity, simply because they are adding to their own tolls and fares by doing so."[1]

This is, no doubt, a fair statement of what connecting roads may be compelled by legislation to do, in the absence of the exclusive right of transportation conferred upon the companies by charter contract. But special legislation upon the subject is probably necessary, even where no exclusive privileges have been conferred.

For it has been decided,[2] that in the absence of legislation requiring it, one railroad company cannot compel a connecting road to enter into joint through-traffic arrangements with it, of the character above described. And this is so, even though the latter road has such

---

[1] Va. R. R. Comm. Report for 1878, p. 11.
[2] A., T., & S. R. R. Co. vs. D. & N. O. R. R. Co., 110 U. S., 667.

arrangements, by contract, with a rival and competitor of the former. In the case where this question was decided, the rights of the parties were governed by the general common law of the country, and by certain constitutional provisions of the State of Colorado. One of these provisions was that: " All individuals, associations, and corporations shall have equal rights to have persons and property transported over any railroads in this State, and no undue or unreasonable discrimination shall be made in charges or facilities for transportation of freight or passengers within the State, and no railroad company, or any lessee, manager, or employé thereof, shall give any preference to individuals, associations, or corporations, in furnishing cars or motive power." Another provision was that: " Every railroad company shall have a right with its road to intersect, connect with, or cross any other railroad."

Of the first constitutional provision, the Court said that it was merely declaratory of the common law. Of the second it was said that it referred only to a physical connection of the tracks of the railroads, and not to a business connection between the companies. " A railroad is prohibited both by the common law and by the constitution of Colorado from discriminating unreasonably in favor of or against another company seeking to do business on its road, but that does not necessarily imply that it must stop at the junction of one road and interchange business there, because it has provided joint depot accommodations, and provided facilities for doing a connecting business with another company at another place." And " the right to do a through business does not necessarily follow from a connection of tracks. The connection may enable the companies to do such a business conveniently, when it is established, but it does not of itself establish the business." But it was distinctly declared that "*such matters are and always have been proper subjects for legislative consideration, unless prevented by some charter contract.*" And "whether a connecting business shall be done over the roads, after the union [of the tracks] is made, depends on *legislative regulation*, or contract obligation." It is true that the remarks of the Court in this case, concerning the powers of the legislature were not strictly necessary for the decision, yet they appear to express the deliberate judgment and opinion of the judges. Reference was made to the English " Railway and Canal Traffic Act," which enjoins upon such carriers the duty of interchange of traffic among themselves without discrimination or preference, and of that it was said : " If complaint was made of a violation of this provision, application could be made to the courts for relief. Were there such a statute in Colorado, this case would come before us in a different aspect."

Reference was also made to a constitutional provision of Pennsylvania, which is as follows : " Every railroad company shall have the right with its road to intersect, connect with, or cross any other railroad ; and shall receive and transport each the other's passengers, tonnage, and cars, loaded or empty, without delay or discrimination."

The Court, by manifest implication, gave its sanction to this constitutional provision, which was cited to show the difference between language which would establish a business connection between connecting companies, and that of the Colorado constitution, which was held to authorize a physical connection merely. A constitutional requirement of a State having the effect to impair an existing contract right, would be quite as vain as an ordinary legislative act having the same object in view. And in the absence of any contract right to the contrary, there is no reason why an act of the legislature may not impose upon railroad companies already created, and whose works are in operation, as well as upon such as are afterwards to be created, the duty of a free interchange of traffic and transportation of each other's cars. The terms upon which connecting roads shall interchange traffic in this way involve inquiries which are judicial in their nature, and if the companies cannot agree among themselves, they should be referred to judicial determination. And there are some important details necessary for the most convenient interchange, which, depending as they do upon contracts entirely, perhaps cannot be required by legislation or enforced by courts. It clearly appears, however, that in the absence of charter contract-rights to the contrary, railway companies may be compelled by legislation to carry along their lines the cars of connecting roads without breaking bulk, or transferring the contents from the vehicles of one company to those of another; or, in other words, to interchange traffic. It is in fact the opinion of some State courts of high authority, that the duty of drawing the cars of connecting roads exists independently of statute,[1] and this opinion certainly conforms logically to the original theory of the railway, which never contemplated an exclusive right to the use of the track. And it seems to be a fair inference that this power of the Legislature, unless limited by contract, may be applied to compel railroad companies to carry over their lines the vehicles and cars, not only of other railroads, but of express companies, or any other persons.[2] In practice cars belonging to private persons are often carried. All these legislative powers over the mode of use of railways—that is, whether the same shall be wholly or partially exclusive, or whether the use of the track shall be open to all comers on the same terms—are referrible to the principle of the "public highway." Unless the exercise of these powers has been limited by the express terms of a binding charter-contract, they may be applied by the legislature as may be deemed most conducive to the public good. Due provision, of course, should always be made to secure to the owners of the road a reasonable compensation for its use, whatever the particular "mode of use" may be.

---

[1] See "Redfield Railways," vol. ii., p. 16 n. (a), and "Harper's Law of Interstate Commerce," p. 151, for authorities.

[2] See Express Cases, 117 U. S., on pp. 28, 29.

But the right of public regulation of the business, and the charges of railroad companies, is derived not alone from the fact that railroads are in their nature public highways, and that the companies owe their existence to an exercise of legislative will, as evidenced in their charters of incorporation ; but also from the public character of the uses to which their property is devoted. This principle was laid down and established as the basis and rationale of legislative authority in the celebrated Granger cases.[1] The leading one of these cases, viz., Munn *vs.* Illinois, did not involve any question of authority over the rates or the transactions of railways or other chartered companies, nor had the power of eminent domain been granted or exercised in aid of the business which was regulated. But the power of a State legislature was affirmed and established, to fix maximum rates for the storage of grain in warehouses, which had been built by private citizens on their own land, and had, theretofore, been controlled by the owners at their will, in respect to the charges and the regulations for their use. A very strong and logical argument against the legislation referred to is contained in the dissenting opinion of Justice Field, with whom Justice Strong concurred. He maintained that legislative power to control the price of the use of property is substantially the power to deprive the owner of his property without due process of law, which is forbidden to the States by the 14th Amendment to the Constitution of the United States.

---

[1] Reported in 94 U. S., from p. 113 to 187.

The majority of the Court, however, speaking through Chief-Justice Waite, said, "that down to the time of the adoption of the 14th Amendment, it was not supposed that statutes regulating the use, or even the price of the use, of private property necessarily deprived an owner of his property, without due process of law. Under some circumstances they may, but not under all.

"The amendment does not change the law in this particular; it simply prevents the States from doing that which will operate as such a deprivation. . . . When private property is affected with a public interest, it ceases to be *juris privati* only. . . . Property does become clothed with a public interest when used in a manner to make it of public consequence, and affect the community at large. When, therefore, one devotes his property to a use in which the public has an interest, he in effect grants to the public an interest in that use, and must submit to be controlled by the public to the extent of the interest he has thus created." Referring then to the circumstances surrounding the business of the warehouses and grain elevators of Chicago, it was said : " Certainly if any business can be clothed with a public interest, and cease to be *juris privati* only, this has been. It may not be made so by the operation of the constitution of Illinois, or by this statute, but it is by the facts. It presents, therefore, a case for the application of a long-known and well established principle of social science, and this statute simply extends the law to meet this new development of commercial progress."

It had been insisted in the argument of the case that the owner of property is entitled to a reasonable compensation for its use, even though it be clothed with a public interest, and that what is reasonable is a judicial and not a legislative question. To this argument the Court replied: " In countries where the common law prevails, it has been customary, from time immemorial, for the legislature to declare what shall be a reasonable compensation under such circumstances, or perhaps, more properly speaking, to fix a maximum, beyond which any charge made would be unreasonable. Undoubtedly, in mere private contracts, in which the public has no interest, what is reasonable must be ascertained judicially. But this is because the legislature has no control over such a contract."

It is apparent, from the reasoning of the decision in this case, that the right of public control over the price of services is based not upon any special privilege or franchise granted to the party rendering them, nor upon the right of the public to have the benefit of such services; for it is distinctly declared that the person exercising the employment may at any time discontinue it.

But it is, as Justice Field remarked, "clear that the Court intended to declare, that whenever one devotes his property to a business which is useful to the public— 'affects the community at large,'—the legislature can regulate the compensation which the owner may receive for its use, and for his own services in connection with it."

The extent of the business then, and the number of people to whom it is useful, together with its character of a practical monopoly, constitute the criterion of the right of public control, and this being the case, the question would seem to be largely one of fact, and sometimes most difficult of correct decision.¹

As said by Judge Cooley, commenting on the case of Munn *vs.* Illinois, in his work on " Constitutional Limitations ² ": " What circumstances shall affect property with a public interest is not very clear. The mere fact that the public have an interest in the existence of the business and are accommodated by it cannot be sufficient, for that would subject the stock of the merchant and his charges to public regulation. The public have an interest in every business in which an individual offers his wares, his merchandise, his services or his accommodations to the public ; but his offer does not place him at the mercy of the public in respect to charges and prices. If one is permitted to take upon himself a public employment, with special privileges which only the State can confer upon him, the case is clear enough ; and it seems to have been the view of both courts in this case that the circumstances were such as to give the warehousemen in Chicago, who were the only persons affected by the legislation, a ' virtual ' monopoly of the business of receiving and forwarding the grain of the country to and from that important point,

---

¹ See some suggestions on this subject in testimony taken by Senate Committee on Labor and Capital, vol. ii., p. 1300.

² Cooley's " Constitutional Limitations," p. 737, 5th edition.

and by the very fact of monopoly to give their business a public character, affect the property in it with a public interest, and make regulation of charges indispensable."

No difficulties from this source arise, however, in the application of the doctrine to the rates of railway transportation, or to the general management and operation of railroads, as there can be no question of the general and pervasive interest the whole public has in their use ; and an additional basis of the right of public control in these cases is found in the fact that the railroad companies exercise their functions and derive their rights and their very existence from the public grants contained in their charters, including the high prerogative franchise of eminent domain.

Thus being the creatures of legislative power they are, in the popular phrase, subject at all times to the regulation and control of their creator. Or, as said by the Supreme Court of the United States [1]: "Railroads are carriers for hire. They are incorporated as such, and given extraordinary powers in order that they may the better serve the public in that capacity. They are, therefore, engaged in a public employment affecting the public interests, and under the decision in Munn vs. Illinois, subject to legislative control as to their rates of fare and freight unless protected by their charters." And not only may the State legislature itself fix maximum rates upon railroads, and otherwise regulate their charges, but it may delegate its

---

[1] C., B., & Q. R. R. Co. vs. Iowa, 94 U. S., p. 155.

powers for that purpose and for many others. For example, in 1884, the legislature of Mississippi passed "an act to provide for the regulation of freight and passenger rates on railroads in the State, and to create a commission to supervise the same, and for other purposes." The railroad companies of the State were required to furnish this commission with their tariffs of charges of every kind. And it was made the duty of the commission " to revise said tariff of charges so furnished, and determine whether or not, and in what particular, if any, said charges are more than just compensation for the services to be rendered, and whether or not unjust discrimination is made in such tariff of charges against any person, locality, or corporation. . . . but in revising any and every tariff of charges, it shall be the duty of said commission to take into consideration the character and nature of the services to be performed, and the entire business of such railroad, together with its earnings from the passenger and other traffic, and so revise such tariff as to allow a fair and just return on the value of such railroad, its appurtenances and equipment." And the commission was empowered to increase or reduce railroad rates as experience and business operations might show to be just, and to fix tariffs of rates for such railroads as should refuse to furnish their tariffs as required by law. Obedience to the requirements of the commission was secured under a penalty, recoverable by action in the name of the State to be instituted by the District Attorney ; and it was provided that "in all trials of cases brought for a violation of any tariff of charges as fixed by the commission, it may be shown in defense that any tariff so fixed is unjust." The legislature thus delegated to the commission its own power to control railroad rates, with the limitation that the rates to be fixed should be such as to yield a fair income on the value of the company's property, and that the justness of the rates fixed should ultimately be determined in the regular courts. And this legislation was sustained by the Supreme Court of the United States.[1] An analysis of the powers of the commission, and of the duties and liabilities of the carriers under the Mississippi act, will show that the latter (that is, the carrier's duties and liabilities) are not greatly changed in respect of their charges from those imposed upon them by the common law,—independent of any contract right to control absolutely their own charges. By the common law a carrier is bound to transport freight and passengers for a reasonable compensation, without unjust discrimination or favoritism.

By reasonable compensation must be meant such compensation as will pay him for his services and afford a fair return of profit on the value of his capital invested in the business; and what is reasonable is a judicial question to be decided in the courts.

By the Mississippi act the commission, it is true, are authorized to fix the carrier's charges, but they are limited by the requirement that they shall so fix them as to

---

[1] Railroad Commission cases, 116 U. S., p. 307.

allow the carrier a fair return on the value of his property—that is, the charges fixed shall be reasonable to the carrier as well as to the public. And the carrier may always show to the court that the charges fixed by the commission are unjust *to him*—that is, the question of reasonableness is still left a judicial one to be ultimately determined in the courts. The principal changes in the common law wrought by the Mississippi act seem to be, first, that the burden of any litigation necessary to enforce the rights of the shipper against the carrier, as those rights are declared by the commission, is assumed by the State on the shipper's behalf; and, second, that the burden of proof is shifted from the shipper, who at the common law would have to verify his complaint, to the carrier, who under the statute has to prove that the rates he is allowed by the commission to charge, are too low or unjust to him. The right to a reasonable compensation is expressly reserved to the carrier, and the conclusions of the commission are not final, but may be reversed in the courts. The rights of the parties are not changed, nor the forum in which they are to be finally adjudicated; only the mode of ascertaining and enforcing their rights is altered. The act effects no change in the property rights of the railway companies, for they were always limited by the rule of reasonable charges. It merely provides machinery for the better administration of the law, and its application to complicated questions.

Besides the powers of the legislatures over railroads and

railroad companies, which are derived from the nature of the road itself as a public highway, and from the public character of the uses to which their property is devoted, there is a very large class of cases where the authority of the public is referrible to the "*police powers*" inherent in every sovereignty. Such are questions of convenience of stations, speed of trains, safety of bridges, approved danger-signals, appliances for safety in car-heating, and in checking or controlling trains in motion, and a vast number and variety of other matters.

These are scarcely within the range of this discussion, which is intended to apply to the question of transportation in its *commercial bearings*.

The police powers, properly so called, are undoubtedly applicable wherever the comfort, convenience, and safety of the public may require; and it is probably beyond legislative power to surrender them by contract.

It has been noticed in the preceding pages, however, that the power of the legislature over the "mode of use" of railways may probably be surrendered by granting to a company the exclusive right of transportation over its own road. And the power over the "price of the use" may also be bargained away by charter contracts, and lost to the public, so long as those contracts remain in force.

CHAPTER II.

Limitation on Legislative Power Arising from Charter Contracts —Strictly Construed against the Corporations—Not Binding where Power to Amend, Alter, or Repeal Charters is Reserved to the Legislature—Examples of Application of the Power to Amend, Alter, or Repeal—Dual Character of Railroad Property Considered — Private Ownership Restricted to Public Use—Right of Public Use Paramount to Private Ownership.

THE limitations imposed upon the right of public regulation of railways by the terms of the contracts contained in their charters (or in a general law in force at the time) deserve further consideration; for, as observed by the Supreme Court: " It is now too late to contend that the charter of a corporation is not a contract within the meaning of that clause of the Constitution of the United States which forbids a State from passing any law impairing the obligation of a contract."[1] The main difficulties under this head of contract exemption from legislative control, consist in determining what language or expressions amount to or constitute a contract between any given railroad company and the public, that the latter will not interfere with or undertake to control the rates or opera-

---

[1] C., B., & Q. R. R. *vs.* Iowa, 94 U. S., 155.

tions of the former. In the case last referred to it was decided that a charter merely authorizing the company to contract in reference to its business of transportation as a natural person might do, and to establish by-laws and make all rules and regulations deemed expedient, does not amount to a contract against a legislative reduction of rates. "This company," it was said, "in the transactions of its business, has the same rights and is subject to the same control as private individuals under the same circumstances. It must carry when called upon to do so, and can charge only a reasonable sum for the carriage. In the absence of any legislative regulations upon the subject, the courts must decide for it, as they do for private persons when controversies arise, what is reasonable; but when the legislature steps in and prescribes a maximum of charge, it operates upon this corporation the same as it does upon individuals engaged in a similar business."

In another case [1] it was held that a provision in the charter that the company should be "bound to carry freight and passengers upon reasonable terms," added nothing to and took nothing from its general liability as a common carrier, and did not at all affect the right of legislative control over the companies' rates. Even where the charter expressly confers on the company power to fix rates, but does not prescribe any maximum, still no contract against legislative control over its rates is created, and such control may be exercised as freely as if the

---

[1] R. R. Co. vs. Blake, 94 U. S., p. 180.

charter did not confer the power.'¹ "This power of regulation is a power of government continuing in its nature, and if it can be bargained away at all, it can only be done by words of positive grant, or something which is equivalent in law. In the words of Chief-Justice Marshall, in Providence Bank *vs.* Billings, 4 Pet., 514, 561, 'its abandonment ought not to be presumed in a case in which the deliberate purpose of the State to abandon it does not appear.' . . . The case turns consequently on Section 12 [of the charter of the company], which is 'that it shall be lawful for the company . . . from time to time to fix, regulate, and receive the tolls and charges by them to be received for transportation,' etc. This would have been implied from the rest of the charter had there been no such provision, and it is argued that unless it had been intended to surrender the power of control over fares and freights, this section would not have been inserted. The argument concedes that the power of the company under this section is limited by the rule of the common law which requires all charges to be reasonable. . . . The claim now is that by Section 12 the State has surrendered the power to fix a maximum for this company, and has declared that the courts shall be left to determine what is reasonable, free of all legislative control. We see no evidence of any such intention. Power is granted to fix reasonable charges, but what shall be deemed reasonable in law is nowhere indicated.

---

¹ R. R. Commission cases, 116 U. S., p. 307.

There is no rate specified nor any limit set. Nothing whatever is said of the way in which the question of reasonableness is to be settled. All that is left as it was. Consequently all the power which the State had in the matter before the charter, it retained afterwards. The power to charge, being coupled with the condition that the charge shall be reasonable, the State is left free to act on the subject of reasonableness, within the limits of its general authority, as circumstances may require. The right to fix reasonable charges has been granted, but the power of declaring what shall be deemed reasonable has not been surrendered. If there had been an intention of surrendering this power, it would have been easy to say so. Not having said so, the conclusive presumption is there was no such intention."

It has recently been decided by the Supreme Court of the United States,[1] that the fixing of maximum rates (that is, providing either in the charter or in a general law applicable to the charter, that the company may charge not exceeding certain specified rates), does not alone amount to a contract protecting against future reduction of rates, below the maximum, by public authority. "It would require much clearer language than this," said the Court, "to justify us in holding that notwithstanding any altered conditions of the country in the future the legislature had, in 1833, contracted that the company might, for all time, charge rates for transportation of

---

[1] R. R. Co. vs. Smith, 9 S. Ct. Reporter, 47.

persons and property over its line up to the limits there designated." An examination of the cases above referred to will show a manifest disposition on the part of the Supreme Court to take hold of any language in charters which offers to sustain an opinion against a surrender of legislative power. This indeed is a fundamental rule of construction of all statutes in derogation of public authority,[1] and the reasoning in the "Railroad Commission Cases," above quoted from, may seem to some rather strained to the same end. It is suggestive that in no case has the claim to exemption from legislative control over traffic charges been sustained by the Supreme Federal Court (though often asserted), on the ground of contract in railway charters.

But where the language permitting charges not exceeding a specified maximum is followed, as is frequently the case, by a stipulation against a legislative reduction of rates in the future, it is difficult to escape from the conviction that a legislative contract is created, the obligation of which the courts will not permit to be impaired.

It can readily be seen that the grant of these special privileges (giving the exclusive right of transportation over the road and limiting the charges only by maximum rates which improvements in construction and management have rendered exorbitant) confers on a railroad company —theoretically at least—very dangerous powers. Accordingly, of late years, the right to amend, alter, and

---

[1] See Charles Riv. Brdg. Co. *vs.* Warren Brdg. Co., 11 Pet., 544.

repeal charters has frequently been reserved by legislative and constitutional provisions. These confer plenary powers over companies subsequently created, but of course they are not retroactive and do not affect contracts contained in the charters of existing corporations. Yet two or more companies, which by virtue of such contracts enjoy more or less immunity from public control, may sometimes by an act of consolidation become incorporated into a new company, and thus lose their special privileges in the operation of the same property. Whether by or under an act of consolidation a new corporation is created out of the consolidated companies, depends upon the legislative intention as manifested in the act. Consolidation does not always or necessarily create a new company. On the contrary, the presumption of law is against the creation of a new corporation by the consolidation.[1] But a legislative act authorizing a consolidation frequently creates a new corporation, and endows it, either directly or indirectly, with corporate powers. Whether these corporate powers be the same, or different from those of the constituent corporations, is immaterial, provided an entirely new and distinct corporation is created and endowed as such with powers of its own. The consolidation may not take place, and the new corporation consequently may not come into being until long after the date of the act authorizing the consolidation; and the powers, privileges, and immunities of the new corporation are determined by

---

[1] Central Railroad Co. *vs.* Georgia, 92 U. S., 665.

the laws in force when it first actually comes into being. And if at that time there is in force any general statutory or constitutional provision against granting special privileges or immunities to corporations, or authorizing the legislature to amend, alter, or repeal their charters, under these circumstances their special privileges may at any time be taken from the new corporations, and regulations contrary thereto imposed upon them. And this is equally true, although by the act of consolidation the new corporation may be expressly endowed, with the franchises, privileges, and immunities of its constituent corporations; for it takes those rights subject to the law as it is when they are given to it. The material facts are the coming into being of a new corporation, and the existence at that time of the general power of amendment, alteration, and repeal.[1]

The same consequences follow where, by any other means, the old corporation is dissolved and a new corporation created, and endowed with the property, rights, franchises, and privileges of the old. Thus it is sometimes provided by law that where a railroad is sold under a mortgage, or decree of court, and a conveyance made to the purchaser, the old company shall, upon the making of such conveyance, *ipso facto* be dissolved, and the purchaser forthwith be a corporation, entitled to all the rights, privileges, and franchises of the old corporation and sub-

---

[1] See Railroad Co. *vs.* Georgia, 98 U. S., 359. Railroad Co. *vs.* Berry, 113 U. S., 465. Shields *vs.* Ohio, 95 U. S., 319.

ject to all its duties. In such cases by the very terms of the law a new corporation is created, and as such powers of its own are granted to it.

"It can in no sense be regarded as the identical corporate body of which it became the successor, merely discharged by a process of insolvency from a further liability for past debts." And though its powers and rights be identical with those of the defunct corporation, and are to be ascertained by reference to the powers which it enjoyed, yet they are as much "granted" by the legislature to the new corporation, as if it had been created by a special act, and its rights, franchises, immunities, and privileges specially declared therein. It is therefore subject to the amending, altering, or repealing power of the legislature in force at the time, and liable to regulative laws, from which the old corporation might have been exempt, by virtue of charter contracts.[1]

It is to be observed, too, that where a specially privileged corporation gets control of other railways, by lease, merger, or consolidation, it does not retain its special privileges in the ownership, operation, and control of the newly acquired property. It acquires no greater rights over or in respect to that property than the old corporation had. So far as its relation to the public in respect to its newly acquired property is concerned, it enjoys the franchises of the old company only. Where legislative powers existed over, or in respect to, the property before

---

[1] C. & O. R. R. Co. vs. Miller, 114 U. S., p. 176.

the merger or consolidation, they exist to the same extent afterwards, unless it is otherwise provided.[1]

On the other hand, the mere consolidation does not divest special privileges, nor enable the legislature to withdraw them (where they were before irrevocable), unless the power to amend, alter, or repeal exists at the time of the consolidation. " When two railroads unite or become consolidated under the authority of law, the presumption is, until the contrary appears, that the united or consolidated company has all the powers and privileges, and is subject to all the restrictions and liabilities of those out of which it was created." [2]

The extent of legislative power over railroad companies, under the reserved right to amend, alter, or repeal charters, taken in connection with the right of eminent domain, seems to have no limit save that imposed upon the exercise of the latter power alone. For example, in 1867, the legislature of Massachusetts chartered the Marginal Freight Railroad Company to operate a street railway in the city of Boston. Subsequently, in 1872, the legislature repealed the charter of the Marginal Company, and incorporated the Union Freight Railroad Company, and authorized the latter to take possession of the tracks of the former upon making compensation. This was resisted on the ground that the act authorizing it was beyond the power of the legislature, and repugnant

---

[1] Tomlinson *vs.* Branch, 15 Wall, 460.
[2] Tennessee *vs.* Whitworth, 117 U. S., 139.

to the Federal Constitution. The Supreme Court said the act would be void unless made valid by the provision of the Massachusetts statutes called "the reservation clause," concerning acts of incorporation.[1] This provision was that every act of incorporation "shall be subject to amendment, alteration, or repeal at the pleasure of the legislature." "What is it may be repealed?" said the Court. "It is the act of incorporation. It is this organic law on which the existence of the company depends, which may be repealed, so that it shall cease to be a law. . . . All this may be done at the pleasure of the legislature. That body need give no reason for its action in the matter. The validity of such action does not depend on the necessity for it, or on the soundness of the reasons which prompted it." Property acquired by a corporation while in existence still belongs to its stockholders after the corporation has ceased to exist, and its contracts remain unimpaired by the repeal of its charter. But "the property of corporations, even including their franchises when that is necessary, may be taken for public use under the power of eminent domain, upon making due compensation." And "it was therefore in the power of the Massachusetts legislature to grant to another corporation, as it did, the authority to operate a street railroad through the same streets and over the same ground previously occupied by the Marginal Company."

Though only a street railway was involved in the de-

---

[1] Greenwood vs. Freight Co., 105 U. S., p. 13.

cision above quoted from, the principles apply to any chartered railroad company, and enable the legislature, under the reserved power to repeal charters, to take away its franchises, and, on payment of just compensation, to bestow its property on others. It will be observed that the extinction of the Marginal Company, and the transfer of its property to the Union Company, were accomplished by legislation derived from two different and distinct sources of legislative power. The extinction of the first corporation was effected by virtue of the right reserved by the legislature to repeal charters; while the transfer of its property to the other corporation was effected under the prerogative power of eminent domain inherent in every sovereignty. The one may be exercised without the payment of any compensation to the corporation or its members; the other can only be exercised upon the payment of just compensation to the owners of the property. It has been seen, though, that the franchises of a corporation are as much subjects of the power of eminent domain as any other property; and the right to be a corporation is itself the fundamental and primary franchise of all these legal entities. So are the rights of corporations as to their rates, exclusive transportation over their roads, and other matters, merely franchises. They may be franchises irrevocable by the legislature, except in the exercise of the power of eminent domain; but no reason is seen why they are not as much subject to that right as any other franchise or property. Of course, where such franchises are so taken, their value must be paid to the parties deprived of their use ; and their value may be largely affected by their exclusive and irrevocable character. Still, on payment of just compensation, they may be taken away. It does not follow either that the exclusive and irrevocable franchises so taken from one corporation must necessarily be vested in the corporation which by virtue of the power of eminent domain takes the property of the former. The franchises of the latter may be limited or subject to repeal, while the exclusive and special privileges, as well as the very being of the former, may by this means be extinguished. This suggests a method by which even the exclusive and vested contract-rights of railroad companies may be constitutionally extinguished by legislative action, whenever the public good may demand it, and their functions conferred upon others more amenable to legislative control.

The expressly reserved power to amend or alter charters has been applied by the Supreme Court of South Carolina, to sustain the validity of a law which imposed upon the railroad companies of the State the expenses of the railroad commission, including the commissioners' salaries.[1]

The right (or power) of the State to impose upon corporations within its jurisdiction the expenses attendant upon public regulation of their business and operations, is also deducible from another and distinct principle, which was clearly laid down by the Supreme Court of Ohio.[2]

The question arose upon a statute of that State creating

---

[1] See R. R. Co. *vs.* Gibbes, 24 S. Car. Repts., p. 60.
[2] See Gas Cos. *vs.* State, 18 Ohio State Repts., p. 237.

the office of gas-inspector, and assessing upon the gas companies of the State an amount sufficient to pay the salary of the officer and expenses of the office.

The gas companies resisted the enforcement of the law, on the ground that it imposed on them a tax additional to that already imposed upon them in common with other persons and corporations, which they contended was in contravention of the State constitution requiring all taxation to be equal. The court, however, construed this constitutional provision to refer to taxation for *general* public purposes, and not to a special assessment to meet expenses attendant upon public supervision of the subject of the assessment. The analogy of inspection laws was pointed out, where the dealer whose goods are inspected pays the inspector's fee, though the inspection is not solicited by him, but forced upon him by law. The subjects of the regulation and of the assessment must, however, be identical,—else the assessment will be void. Upon this ground a statute of Kansas, intended to regulate *express* and railroad companies, but assessing the latter alone with the expenses, was held invalid by the Supreme Court of that State.[1] The general question of the power of the State to impose on railway companies the expenses of their regulation has not, however, been the subject of adjudication in the United States Supreme Court,—before which it may almost certainly be brought, —and, therefore, cannot be considered as settled.

---

[1] See 32 Kansas Reports, p. 737.

In considering the extent of legislative power over railroad transportation, the dual character of railway property must be constantly and clearly borne in mind, to wit, that of *private ownership*, restricted to *public use*.

By public use is not necessarily meant that all persons shall have the use of the road for their cars and motive power, for that, as has been shown, is a matter of legislative discretion, in the absence of contracts forbidding its exercise. The use may, and must, still be public, even though the legislature has granted to the railroad company the exclusive right of transportation over its own line. And the public use is enjoyed under these circumstances only when the railroad company furnishes equal facilities to all alike, and practises no *unjust* discrimination against any kind of traffic, any locality, or any person. If a railroad company for purposes of profit, or from any other motive whatever, declines or fails to furnish equal facilities to all, or discriminates *unjustly* or *unreasonably* against any kind of traffic, or any locality, or any person, it thereby perverts the use of its railroad from public to private ends.

In doing this it violates the fundamental constitution and object of its existence. There can be no doubt that the right of public use of the railroad is paramount to the right of private property in it, and where the circumstances are such that either the public use, as above described, must be denied, or the private profits must be curtailed, the latter result must follow, and not the former.

This doctrine is carried to the extent that a court will sometimes direct the operation of a railroad in the hands of a receiver, under circumstances that will probably entail a loss on security holders, in order that the public may have the benefit of its use as a highway for trade and travel. "A railroad is authorized to be constructed more for the public good to be subserved than for private gain. As a highway for public transportation, it is a matter of public concern, and its construction and management belong primarily to the commonwealth, and are only put into private hands to subserve the public convenience and economy. But the public retains rights of vast consequence in the road and its appendages, with which neither the company nor any creditor or mortgagee can interfere. They take their rights, subject to the rights of the public, and must be content to enjoy them in subordination thereto."[1] This is a necessary consequence of the public character of railroads and the object for which their construction was authorized by the grant of their high and important franchises. That object, or at all events the prime object, was the general good of the whole public. Upon this ground alone have many of their most important rights and privileges been sustained. This has already been abundantly shown. Of course, the promoters and incorporators of railroad enterprises undertake them for their private gain and profit, and this they un-

---

[1] Barton *vs.* Barbour, 104 U. S., p. 135. Referred to approvingly in Mittenberger *vs.* R. R. Co., 106 U. S., p. 312.

doubtedly should have, if it can be made by the operation of their works consistently with the public welfare, but not otherwise. The State says to the incorporators: "Take the citizen's land whether he will or no. Receive public donations offered you by cities or counties, even against the will of a large minority of those who are taxed to raise those donations. Build your road, and make out of it what legitimate profit you can. But remember I give you this power for the general good of all the people, and you must not in its use pervert it from that object. If, confining the power granted you to that object, you make great profit, well! But if profit fail to accrue from such use of your franchises, you must not for your private gain pervert them from that object, to the injury of any portion of the community. This is the essential condition of my grant." This language is implied in every railroad charter, unless expressly excluded by the use of other language, clearly conferring other rights. The incorporators take their rights subject to those conditions, and no vested rights are impaired by subsequent legislation, restraining them to the legitimate use of their franchises. This indeed is true of all corporations. Even of an insurance company it has been authoritatively declared[1] that its right " to exist as a corporation, and its authority in that capacity to conduct the particular business for which it was created, were granted, subject to the condition that the privileges and franchises conferred upon it should not be

---

[1] Chicago Life Ins. Co. vs. Needles, 113 U. S., p. 580.

abused, or so employed as to defeat the ends for which it was established, and when so abused or misemployed, they might be withdrawn or reclaimed by the State in such way and by such modes of procedure as were consistent with law. Although no such condition is expressed in the company's charter, it is necessarily implied in every grant of corporate existence. . . . If this condition be not necessarily implied, then the creation of corporations with rights and franchises which do not belong to individual citizens may become dangerous to the public welfare, through the ignorance or misconduct or fraud of those to whose management their affairs are entrusted." How much more applicable this language to a railroad company in the operation of a " public highway "!

It is a fundamental principle too, that where a legislative contract granting special privileges to a railroad company exists and is valid, it must always be most strictly construed against the company. The power of railway regulation is a power of government continuing in its nature, and if there is reasonable doubt whether the power has been surrendered, it must be resolved in favor of the existence of the power.[1] A legislative contract therefore permitting a railroad company to charge certain specified rates, and binding the legislature not to reduce them, does not authorize discriminations in charges to be made by the company, even though both the highest and the lowest rates charged are within the maximum allowed by law.

---

[1] See R. R. Commission cases *supra*.

Legislation against unjust discrimination may be enacted, and would almost certainly be held valid, notwithstanding such contract as to rates. So a company which has the exclusive right of transportation over its road, may be prohibited from unjustly discriminating between connecting roads, in giving them the use of its track, hauling or refusing to haul their cars, or in any particular connected with the interchange of traffic.

It does not follow though, that discriminations, if made, must necessarily be unjust. In fact, discrimination in charges, under certain circumstances, seems to be absolutely essential to the public good. And legislation against discrimination of this character, though valid so far as contract obligations are concerned, may frequently operate to deprive a railroad company of a portion at least of its net revenues, without in any manner benefiting any of the communities which it serves. Under these circumstances, such legislation amounts to an arbitrary taking of private property, without accomplishing any public good, and could scarcely receive judicial sanction.

CHAPTER III.

Limitation on Legislative Power Arising from the Private Property Rights of Owners of Railways, or Railway Securities—Power to Regulate Railway Charges, Analogous to Power of Eminent Domain—Can only be Exercised for the Accomplishment of Some Public Good, and must not Deprive Owners of Reasonable Income on Just Value of Property—Just Value Distinguished from Capitalization—Regulation not Equivalent to Confiscation—Distinction between Charges Fixed by Public Authority for Specific Services, and the Entire Schedule of Rates as a Whole—The Latter Ultimately Subject to Judicial Revision—The Tilley Case (U. S. Circuit Court in Georgia) and Cases from Supreme Court Compared—Recent Iowa Cases.

THE Fourteenth Amendment to the Federal Constitution provides that no State shall "deprive any person of life, liberty, or property, without due process of law, nor deny to any person within its jurisdiction the equal protection of the laws."

Of provisions substantially similar to these, it has been said by the Supreme Court of the United States that "the good sense of mankind has at last settled down to this—that they were intended to secure the individual from the arbitrary exercise of the powers of government, unrestrained by the established principles of private rights and distributive justice."[1]

Corporations, or artificial persons are included in the meaning of the constitution as well as individuals or natural persons.[2]

The right of private property in railroads though subordinate to the right of public use, is as clearly entitled to recognition and protection within its limits, as any other private right of property. The Congress of the United States, and the legislatures of perhaps all the States are forbidden by constitutional provisions from exercising the right of eminent domain—that is, from taking private property for public use, except upon making due compensation therefor. The power of eminent domain can only be exercised where the property to be taken is for a public use—that is, where some public good is accomplished or some measure of public benefit promoted. The arbitrary taking of property (and the destruction of revenues therefrom amounts to the same thing) where no public good can be subserved thereby seems never to have been contemplated as being within the limits of governmental power, within the purview of the right of eminent domain. No constitutional limit was therefore necessary to be fixed to a power which was supposed to have no existence at all. And if it be true that no such power exists, the taking of private property or the arbitrary curtailment of private

---

[1] Bank of Columbia vs. Okely., 4 Wheat., 235.
[2] Sinking Fund cases, 99 U. S., p. 718; and Santa Clara Co. vs. R. R. Cos., 118 U. S., p..1.

revenues, where no public good can result from such action, appears to be beyond legislative authority. The right to regulate the price which may be received by the owner for the use of property devoted by him to public service, seems to be analogous to the right of eminent domain. If the analogy is a sound one, the price of such use as fixed by public regulation must be a just compensation therefor, and the regulation can only be exercised in furtherance of the public interest. Extortion and *unjust* discrimination in railway charges and operations are both prejudicial to the public interest, and in the absence of charter rights to the contrary they may undoubtedly be prohibited by legislation. Leaving out of view the question of *discrimination* (which is relative extortion), the practice of general *extortion* by railway companies may be defined as making such charges for services as in the aggregate will swell "net earnings" above what is necessary to pay a fair return on the *just value* of their property. The terms "earnings" and "net earnings," as applied to railroad affairs, have been judicially defined.[1] The former includes all receipts arising from operations as a railroad company, but not those from public lands granted to the company, nor fictitious charges for the transportation of its own property and material.

"Net earnings," within the meaning of the law, are ascertained by deducting from the gross earnings all the ordinary expenses of organization, and of operating the

---

[1] R. R. Co. *vs.* U. S., 99 U. S., p. 402.

road and keeping the property in good condition ; but not deducting interest paid on any of the bonded debt of the company. It is of the highest public consequence that a sufficient amount of the gross earnings should be applied to the maintenance of the roadway, bridges, structures, and equipment generally, in the highest state of efficiency, and to the constant improvement, as far as practicable, of organization and management.

In fact considerably more than one half of the gross earnings are usually so applied. The net earnings of American railroads have in recent years averaged between 35 and 40 per cent. of gross earnings. It is only from these net earnings that a fair return on the just value of the property can be derived by its owners. The just value of railroad property is by no means always or necessarily its capitalized value—that is, the face of the stock and bonds issued upon it. It is notorious that the capitalization frequently aggregates an amount vastly more than the just value of the property, and constitutes no criterion of the reasonableness of charges. This appears from the case of Dow *vs.* Beidelman (125 U. S., 680), which was as follows:

The legislature of Arkansas had prescribed a maximum rate of three cents per mile for the transportation of passengers in that State, over lines of railroads exceeding seventy-five miles in length.

The Memphis & Little Rock Railroad Co., which came within the terms of this legislation, refused to reduce rates to three cents per mile, and was sued for the refusal.

On the trial it was admitted as a fact that the net earnings of the company under the statutory rate would be less than one and a half per cent. on the original cost of its road, and only a little over two per cent. on its bonded indebtedness. The road, however, was not built by the company named, but had been purchased by it at a judicial sale, and the new company had issued its mortgage bonds upon the purchased property bearing eight per cent. interest. The purchase price of the property, or the price paid for the bonds, or the amount of the capital stock of the new company were not disclosed. Under these circumstances the Court was asked to make the following declaration of law: That the act of the Arkansas legislature above referred to was unconstitutional, null, and void, because, under the guise of regulating charges for the carriage of passengers on railroads, it amounted virtually to the confiscation of the property of the railroad, and was an unreasonable, unjust, and oppressive taking of private property for public uses without compensation, and in violation of the constitution. The Supreme Court, while admitting that such legislation might, under some circumstances, be unconstitutional, said: "It certainly can not be presumed that the price paid at the sale, under the decree of foreclosure, equalled the original cost of the road, or the amount of its outstanding bonded debt. Without any proof of the sum invested by the re-organized corporation or its trustees, the court has no means, if it would under any circumstances have the power, of determining that the rate of three cents a mile fixed by the legislature is unreasonable. Still less does it appear that there has been any such confiscation as amounts to a taking of property without due process of law." It is to be observed that the court here entirely disregarded the capitalization as a material element in establishing reasonable charges, and suggested a doubt as to whether even the actual cost to the present owners of the property would constitute a criterion for that purpose. But to affirm, as was done in this case, and in the Granger cases, that the State may reduce railroad charges below the point which will enable the companies to pay interest on bonds and dividends on stock,—or even below the point which will enable them merely to pay full interest on the bonded debt,—is by no means to affirm that the State may reduce charges, so far as to prevent a reasonable net income being earned on the just value of the railway property, treating its entire operation as a single unit. In the Granger cases, the sufficiency of the rates fixed by public authority to yield a reasonable net income on the just value of the property was not discussed ; the controversy being as to the right, or constitutional power of the legislature to interfere at all with railway tariffs. " The great question to be decided, and which was decided, and which was argued in all those cases, was the right of a State, in which a railroad company did business, to regulate or limit the amount of any of these traffic charges." [1]

---

[1] Wabash, &c., R. R. Co. *vs.* Illinois, 118 U. S., 557.

This power is always reserved by government unless expressly surrendered. But it is equally true that "beyond the sphere of the reserved powers, the vested rights of corporations in such cases are surrounded by the same sanctions, and are as inviolable as in other cases."[1] And in connection with the public right of regulating railroads and limiting their charges, it has been declared, by way of qualification, "that it is not to be inferred that this power of regulation or limitation is itself without limit. The power to regulate is not a power to destroy, and limitation is not the equivalent of confiscation. Under pretence of regulating fares and freights, the State can not compel a railroad company to carry persons and property without reward; neither can it do that which amounts in law to a taking of private property for public use, without just compensation, or without due process of law."[2] Now, if the State cannot compel the railroads to carry persons and property without reward, can she compel them to carry at rates which will be inadequate to pay the expense of carrying? If the rates be inadequate to pay the operating expenses, they are really carrying not only without reward, but at a loss. If they are barely enough to pay operating expenses, they are still carrying without reward. It is only when the gross receipts pay more than operating expenses, and expenses of maintaining the property, that any thing is left for the people whose money is represented in the railroad and its equip-

---

[1] Shields vs. Ohio, 95 U. S., 319.
[2] See R. R. Commission cases *ante*.

ment. Then only are they in any just sense carrying for reward. Who, then, is to determine whether the rates will yield income sufficient to reward the company (not merely the employés) for carrying persons and property?

Manifestly the legislature or a commission cannot ultimately determine this question, since, if it had that power, it might recite in a preamble or resolution that a certain schedule of rates would reward the railroad company for its services, and fix that as a maximum of rates, whereas it might be perfectly demonstrable that such a schedule of rates would not even pay operating expenses. This manifestly would be to compel the railroads to carry persons and property without reward.

The question, then, presented in this light, must ultimately become a judicial one. Nor is this conclusion repugnant to the decisions in the Granger cases. In them the question was merely whether the legislature could regulate railway charges at all, and the question whether the regulation denied to the owners of the property a just compensation for its use was not presented. The courts will presume, however, where the legislature or a commission fixes maximum rates, that they are adequate to afford a just compensation for the use of the property. The rates will be presumed to be reasonable to the carrier as well as to the shipper. And in certain cases this presumption is conclusive. This is the case in a controversy between the railroad company and one of its customers over the price of a certain service. The price fixed by statute or by the commission is there conclusive of the rights of the parties, and the company cannot recover more than the statutory price, by showing that the amount claimed would only be a reasonable compensation for the service rendered.[1]

The question of reasonableness in a controversy between the carrier and a single shipper in regard to a single transaction is no longer a judicial one, after the legislature or commission has fixed a rate. But this may be reconciled with the right of the judicial department of the government to inquire into the reasonableness of the schedule of rates as a whole, in a case where the public is substantially a party. And this may be in a proceeding to forfeit the charter of a company for refusing to carry at the statutory rates,[2] or, it would seem, in a suit in equity to injoin the enforcement of the law. Under this view, to make the question a judicial one, the distinct averment must be made in presenting the case of the railroads to the court, that the schedule of rates as a whole, treating the continuous operation of the road as a single unit, will afford no net return, or no just compensation, for the use of the property, estimated at its *just value*, as distinguished from its capitalization.

It does not follow because a single item of transportation is fixed in a legislative schedule of rates at a price which would be unreasonable, if standing alone, that the schedule as a whole is unreasonable. The legislature (or

---

[1] Railroad Co. *vs.* Ackley, 94 U. S., 179.   [2] *Id.*

commission) in fixing rates may—and with good reason—make some items of transportation bear a much less share than others of the expenses etc., in proportion to the cost of the service rendered.

This, in fact, is what the railroad companies constantly do themselves.

And the corporation cannot be heard to object thereto, so long, at least, as the compensation received by it for carriage over its road as a whole is reasonable.[1]

It is the entire schedule of rates and its effect on the earnings, which is a public question, and to that the controversy between the carrier and a single shipper is merely collateral. Hence in such a controversy the rate fixed by law is conclusively presumed to be reasonable, just as a judgment of a court of competent jurisdiction collaterally involved in any suit is conclusively presumed to be right. But as the judgment might be directly impeached as contrary to law, so, it would seem, may an act of legislation, fixing a schedule of railroad rates plainly inadequate to afford a fair revenue, or conferring on a commission unlimited powers for that purpose, be directly impeached as subversive of natural justice and constitutional rights.

Legislation of such a character as that, it could be demonstrated, must necessarily deprive railroad companies of all profit or of a reasonable profit on the *just value* of their property, would certainly be unjustifiable, and would hardly be sustained by the courts, unless in the absence of such

---

[1] *Ex parte* Koeler, 23 Fed. Rep., p. 529.

legislation the public will inevitably sustain grievous and irremediable injury. The same may be said of legislation which confers on a commission, or other legislative agency, unlimited control over railroad charges enforcible by penalties, without providing any redress for the railway companies against injustice in the action of the commission. It has been observed that in the Mississippi law, which was sustained by the Supreme Court,[1] the rights of the companies were carefully guarded in this respect. And the provision for this purpose was alluded to by the court as an answer to the argument that the companies were denied the equal protection of the laws, and might be deprived of their property without due process of law or due compensation therefor. This was the provision that, in all cases where a company might be sued for violating the tariff of rates as fixed by the commission, " it may be shown in defence that any tariff so fixed is unjust."

The advocates of a commission with unlimited powers over railroad companies rely in support of the constitutionality of their views upon the opinion of Justice Woods, of the Supreme Court, delivered in the United States Circuit Court in Georgia.[2] The validity of the Railroad Commission Act of that State was there brought in question, on an application for an injunction to prevent the commissioners from enforcing the law. That act empowered the commissioners to make reasonable and just rates of freight

---

[1] See Railroad Commission cases *ante*.
[2] Tilley *vs.* Railroad Co., 5 Fed. Reporter, 641.

and passenger tariffs for all the railroads in the State, and provided that in all suits brought against the railroads involving their charges or discriminations therein, the schedule of rates fixed by the commission should be deemed and taken as " *sufficient evidence* " that the rates therein fixed are just and reasonable. It was claimed that the law was unconstitutional, because this provision deprived the companies of the right of trial by jury, and denied them the equal protection of the law accorded to other persons. Upon this point Judge Woods said : " In this provision the legislature has exercised the power, exercised by all the legislatures, both Federal and State, of prescribing the effect of evidence, and it has done nothing more.

" Even in criminal cases Congress has declared that certain facts proved shall be evidence of guilt. For instance, in section 3,082 of the United States Revised Statutes, it is provided that whenever on an indictment the defendant is shown to be in possession of smuggled goods, ' such possession shall be deemed evidence sufficient to authorize a conviction, unless the defendant shall explain the possession to the satisfaction of the jury.' The statute-books are full of such acts, but it has never been considered that this impairs the right of trial by jury."

The illustration used by the judge from the Revised Statutes indicates that he construed the expression " sufficient evidence," used in the law, to refer to *prima-facie* evidence merely. Under this construction the objection urged to the provision was manifestly untenable. But if the expression " sufficient evidence " had been held equivalent to " conclusive evidence," it is difficult to see how the objection could have been answered. Under the former construction, the railroads still have the right to resort to the regular tribunals constituted of court and jury for redress against the unjust acts of the commission. Under the latter, they would, so far as the constitutional guaranty of the right of jury trial is of any substantial value, be practically deprived of that right.

In the first case, the burden of justifying their violations of the orders of the commission is imposed upon the railroads; but, in the latter, they are denied the means, or the right, of justifying themselves by any evidence at all, contrary to the views of the commission. In point of fact, in this case, the court did consider the evidence adduced, as to the probable effect upon the revenues of the company of the rates established by the commission, and came to the conclusion (such was the conflict of opinion among witnesses) that the only way of ascertaining the effect would be by actual experiment. The commissioners expressed an entire willingness to change their schedule of rates, should the experiment prove it to be unjust to the railroads. And the Court concluded that: " The railroad company, after testing the results of the schedule of rates fixed by the commission and finding it to be unjust and unreasonable, can apply to the commission for redress. If redress is denied them there, they can apply to the legislature for relief. Believing the law under which the commissioners are appointed to be within the constitutional power of the legislature, the redress must come either from the commissioners or from the General Assembly. It is not in the power of this court to give relief." This language, though not necessary for the decision, may be construed to indicate that, in Judge Woods' opinion, the courts can not interfere to prevent unjust and oppressive action on the part of the commission (unless its powers are limited in terms), no matter how plain the evidence of it may be.

But this view scarcely harmonizes with the reasonable interpretation, and application of the constitutional limitations we are now considering, or with conclusions which seem to be fairly deducible from several remarks (heretofore commented on) which were carefully and purposely made in the delivery of opinions from the supreme bench.

In a case involving a single shipment—an implied contract between the freighter and the railway company,—it is true that no evidence can be received *aliunde* the rate fixed by public authority. But there is nothing in the decisions of the Supreme Court to justify legislation which would deprive the railroads of the right to have tested in the regular judicial tribunals of the country, the question whether rates, fixed either directly by the legislature or by a commission, are not such as, considering the entire operation of the road and not merely isolated transactions with individuals, will compel those operations to be carried on, if at all, at a profit grossly inadequate to the just value of the property, or perhaps at an actual loss. To preclude judicial inquiry into such a question savors strongly of oppression, and of a denial of "equal protection of the laws." It is possible (as may be shown), by prohibiting discriminations, as well as by fixing maximum rates, to deprive a railway company of a portion, at least, of its profits, under circumstances where the enforcement of the prohibition will result in no benefit to the community, but will deprive the company of any adequate return on the just value of its property.

This result may even sometimes follow, from the establishment of an absolute minimum rate, or the adoption of an inflexible rule forbidding a greater aggregate charge for a short than a longer haul, under any circumstances; or from other legislation which, with the purpose of preventing discriminations on the part of railroads, fails to take note of certain circumstances beyond the control of either railroads or the legislature. Under these circumstances, such legislation can scarcely be judicially sustained.

Since this chapter was written the questions here discussed have been elaborately considered in connection with the Iowa Railroad Law of 1888. (See "The Iowa Railroad Case," compiled by H. S. Fairall.) By that the railroad commissioners were empowered and directed to make, for each of the railroad companies doing business in that State, a schedule of reasonable maximum rates and charges for the transportation of freight and cars on each of said roads. The commissioners prepared a schedule and tariff of rates, and were proceeding to put it into effect when certain railroad companies applied both in the Federal and in the State courts for injunctions against the enforcement of the commission's tariff. One of the principal grounds upon which the application was based, was that the schedule of rates prescribed was unreasonably low, and would, if enforced, disable the companies from earning sufficient compensation to pay fixed charges and operating expenses. The State authorities insisted that the courts had no right to inquire whether the schedule was reasonable or not ; and that the commission having fixed a tariff of charges in accordance with the forms of law, all inquiry in the courts was at an end. In each court, however, it was decided that, assuming the truth of the allegation that the tariff as fixed would not afford compensation to the carriers, the enforcement of the tariff might be prevented. Judge Brewer in the Federal court said : " Coming now to the question of the schedule as prepared, I remark that the schedule as a whole must control. And its validity or invalidity does not depend on the sufficiency or insufficiency of the rates on any few particular subjects of transportation. . . . The rule therefore to be laid down is this, that where the proposed rates will give compensation, however small, to the owners of the railroad property, the courts have no power to interfere. Appeal must then be made to the legislature and the people. But where the rates prescribed will not pay some compensation to the owners, then it is the duty of the courts to interfere to protect the companies from such rates. Compensation implies three things: Payment of cost of service, interest on bonds, and then some dividends. . . . While by reducing the rates the value of the stockholders' property may be reduced, in that less dividends are payable (and that power of the legislature over property is conceded), yet if the rates are so reduced that no dividends are possible, and especially if they are such that the interest on the mortgage debt is not earned, then the enforcement of the rates means either confiscation, or compelling, in the language of the Supreme Court, the corporations to carry persons or property without reward." Judge Fairall in the State court said: "It requires no argument to demonstrate the proposition, that to require a common carrier to transport property for less than a just and reasonable charge, is to require him to carry it without reward, and to do what, says Chief-Justice Waite in Farmers' Loan and Trust Co. *vs.* Stone, 116 U. S., 33, 'amounts to a taking of private property for public use without just compensation, or without due process of law.' . . . If, then, as it is evident both on principle and authority, it is not competent for either the legislature or a board acting under it to require a common carrier to transport property without reward, where but in the courts can the complaining party go for redress? . . . The subject of controversy is the compensating use of plaintiff's property, and the value of such property, as a rule, is determined by its earnings. . . . The questions involved in this case are purely legal, and the main one is the power of a State to make and enforce rates of transportation to be charged by railroad companies and other common carriers, when from the pleadings such rates are admitted to be so low as not to pay fixed charges and operating expenses. This question, which has never been squarely determined by the Supreme Court, either of this State or of the United States, is one which must be met by the courts; and passed upon the same as other controverted rights between the State and the individual. There is a line between rates which are compensatory to the carrier, and those which are not; and on principle as well as authority, when complaint is made of an injury to private rights by the acts of public officials, as is alleged in this case, it is, as in all other alleged infringements of such rights, the duty of judicial tribunals to investigate and determine the very right of the matter, whether it involves the validity of a statute, or the legality of the acts of officers acting thereunder."

The conclusion here arrived at, namely, that the question of the reasonableness of a schedule of railroad charges fixed by public authority must ultimately be judicially determined, is irresistible.

But in the decisions just quoted from, opinions are expressed, as to the measure of compensation which the schedules as a whole must furnish, that scarcely appear to be well founded. Thus Judge Brewer distinctly declares that the courts should interfere, where the commissions schedules will disable the companies from paying, 1st, operating expenses ; 2d, interest on bonds ; and 3d, some dividends, however small.

Under this opinion the capitalization of the property is to determine the extent of the compensation to which the company is entitled, with this limitation only, that the stockholder, as distinguished from the bondholder, must be satisfied with the merest pittance, in the shape of a dividend, that the public choose to allow him. This is a most remarkable conclusion, and, logically carried out, would result in this : that a road built and equipped with subscribed money (that is, with the proceeds of its stock, and without any bonded debt), at a cost of say $30,000 per mile, might be compelled to submit to a tariff which, after paying operating expenses, would yield a net income of say $\frac{1}{2}$ of one per cent., or $150 per mile ; while a road having no better, or perhaps less favorable, traffic conditions, built with the proceeds of 6 per cent. bonds to the amount of $30,000 per mile, could not be compelled to accept a tariff which would yield net earnings to a less amount than $1,800 per mile. No such distinction as this can be just. The consideration of the *character* of the capitalization of a road,—that is, whether consisting of bonds or stock,—must necessarily be misleading in coming to a conclusion upon the reasonableness of a schedule of tariff charges. And to a very great extent the *amount* of the capitalization is also immaterial. The cost, as well as the just value, of railroad property, may be something entirely apart from the character and amount of the securities issued against it. The true conclusion seems to be that the corporation (which is a person entirely distinct from either its creditors or its stockholders) is entitled to such a schedule of rates as will enable it to earn operating expenses, and, in addition thereto, a sum which shall be a reasonable income on the just value of its property. And whether this net income be distributed to stockholders or bondholders is entirely immaterial.

In connection with the revisory powers of the courts over legislation intended for the regulation of railroad charges, the case of *ex parte Kochler* (23 Fed. Rep., p. 529) may be referred to. Some of the remarks of the Court in that case are very forcible in support of the views which have been advanced in this chapter. The question involved was the validity of an act of the Oregon legislature, forbidding a greater charge for a shorter than a longer haul; and the Court said : " The question, although *prima facie* one of discrimination, directly involves the right to a reasonable compensation. I assume that the State has the power to prevent a railway company from discriminating between persons and places for the sake of putting one up or another down, or any other reason than the real exigencies of its business. Such discrimination it seems to me is a wanton injustice, and may therefore be prohibited. It violates the fundamental maxim which in effect forbids any one to so use his property as to injure another. . . .'

but where the discrimination is between places only, and is the result of competition with other lines or means of communication, the case I think is different. . . . If the legislature cannot require a railway corporation formed under the laws of the State, to carry freight for nothing, or at any less rate than a reasonable one, then it necessarily follows that this provision of the act, cannot be enforced so far as to prevent the railway from competing with the water craft . . . even if in so doing they are compelled to charge less for a long haul than for a short one in the same direction. It is not the fault or contrivance of the railways that enforces this discrimination, but it is the necessary result of circumstances altogether beyond its control. It is not done wantonly for the purpose of putting the one place up, or the other down, but only to maintain its business against rival and competing lines of transportation."

CHAPTER IV.

Limitation on State Powers Arising from Exclusive Right of Congress to " Regulate Commerce among the States "—Interstate Commerce Defined and Illustrated—States Cannot Regulate Charges Thereon, and Probably Cannot Prevent Traffic Arrangements between its Own and Foreign Corporations in Respect Thereto—But Leases and Consolidations between Domestic and Foreign Corporations, Probably under Control of States and not of Congress—Sources and Limitations of Powers of Congress Discussed.

THE most important limitation, perhaps, upon the powers of the State legislatures in the control of railroad transportation arises where the transportation is from points without the State to points within, or *vice versa;* or where it is entirely through the State, from and to points without. The limitation has its origin in the constitutional provision conferring on Congress the power to regulate commerce among the several States. No doubt seems ever to have been entertained that a State would be precluded by this provision from fixing rates where neither terminus of the transit is within its limits. But where freight is taken up within a State and carried without, or taken up outside and brought within, conflicting views of the regulative powers of the State have until recently been entertained. There are undoubtedly instances in which a State may, in the absence of Congressional action, pass laws which amount to a regulation of commerce among the States. They are usually cases where the direct object of the State legislation is the enforcement of police regulations, and where the effect upon commerce is only incidental. For example, a State may (where Congress has not acted on the subject) compel railroad companies operating within its limits to publish their schedules of rates, and to confine their charges within the published limits, even where the charge is for transportation from or to another State. Such a requirement was unanimously sustained by the Supreme Court as a police regulation.[1]

On substantially similar grounds a State law requiring locomotive engineers to be examined and licensed as such by a public board, as a prerequisite to the pursuit of their calling, has been sustained by the Supreme Court of the United States[2] (the legislation of Congress containing no provision on the subject), although the engineer's regular "run" was between points located in different States.

But national regulations, even on such subjects, will supersede and nullify State laws so far as applicable to interstate commerce.

For, as said by the Court in the case last referred to:

---

[1] Fuller *vs.* Railroad Co., 17 Wall, 560. (Prior to the enactment of the Interstate Commerce Law.)

[2] Smith *vs.* Alabama, 124 U. S., p. 465. (The Alabama law was passed after the Interstate Act, but the latter has no conflicting provision.)

"It would indeed be competent for Congress to . . . prescribe the qualifications of locomotive engineers for employment by carriers engaged in foreign or interstate commerce. It has legislated upon a similar subject by prescribing the qualifications for pilots and engineers of steam vessels engaged in the coasting trade and navigating the inland waters of the United States and such legislation is undoubtedly justified on the ground that it is incident to the power to regulate commerce. . . The power might with equal authority be exercised in prescribing the qualifications for locomotive engineers employed by railroad companies engaged in the transportation of passengers and goods among the States, and in that case would supersede any conflicting provisions on the same subject made by local authority." Nor is a railroad company relieved from State regulation and control simply because it has been incorporated by and is carrying on business in other States through which its road runs. The corporation created by each State is for all the purposes of local government a domestic corporation, and its railroad within the State is a matter of domestic concern. Hence the State may govern such a corporation as it does all domestic corporations as to every act and every thing within the State, which is the lawful subject of State government. It may beyond all question regulate freights and fares for business done exclusively within the State. But nothing can be done by the State which will act as a burden on the interstate commerce of the company, or impair its facilities for interstate traffic.[1] This suggests the inquiry, What is interstate commerce? And the answer is that "whenever a commodity has begun to move as an article of trade from one State to another, commerce in that commodity between the States has commenced. The fact that several different and independent agencies are employed in transporting the commodity, some acting in one State, and some acting through two or more States, does in no respect affect the character of the transaction. To the extent to which each agency acts in that transportation it is subject to the regulation of Congress."[2]

If the authority of Congress "does not extend to an agency in such commerce, when that agency is confined within the limits of a State, its entire authority over interstate commerce may be defeated. Several agencies combining, each taking up the commodity transported at the boundary line at one end of a State, and leaving it at the boundary line at the other end, the Federal jurisdiction would be entirely ousted, and the constitutional provision would become a dead letter."[3] It appears then that the starting-point and the destination of an article of commerce are to be looked to, in order to determine its character as domestic, or interstate, commerce. If the article starts from one State and is destined to another it belongs to interstate commerce, and the means by which

---

[1] See Railroad Commission cases *ante*.
[2] The Daniel Ball, 10 Wall, 557.   [3] *Id.*

it is transported to its place of destination is immaterial, as is also the question whether such transportation is to be continuous and uninterrupted across State lines, or whether the article is to be transferred from one agency or vehicle of transportation to another, at the State line or elsewhere. It is still an article of interstate commerce, and every agency handling it is as to it subject to regulation by Congress. But the mere design and intention or preparation to ship a commodity from one State to another does not bring it within the definition of "commerce among the States." "The point of time when State jurisdiction over the commodities of commerce begins and ends is not an easy matter to define." Articles intended for exportation to another State, and which have even been brought to and deposited at a place of shipment for that purpose, do not become subject to Federal jurisdiction until actually shipped and started on their final journey out of the State. Up to that time the "exportation is a matter altogether *in fieri*, and not at all a fixed and certain thing." But this " does not present the predicament of goods in course of transportation through a State, though detained for a time within the State. . . . Such goods are already in the course of commercial transportation, and are clearly under the protection of the Constitution."[1] Under these principles, for instance, if an Illinois farmer were to ship grain to Chicago, where the products of the State accumulate before their final

---

[1] Coe *vs.* Errol, 116 U. S., 517.

carriage east begins, the shipment would be subject to the regulative laws of the State and not of Congress, although it might amount to a certainty that that very grain would ultimately be forwarded to the seaboard. But if he were to bill the grain directly from his shipping station to New York, then the shipment would be exempt from State regulation even within the limits of the State. This question has only recently been decided by the Supreme Court,[1] and a strong minority of the court dissented from the opinion. The question arose in an action brought by the State of Illinois to recover a penalty for the breach of a statute "to prevent extortion and unjust discrimination in the rates charged for the transportation of passengers and freight on railroads in the State." This statute provided, in substance, that if any railroad company should charge, for the transportation of passengers and freight upon its railroad for any distance within the State, the same or more than is at the same time charged for the transportation in the same direction of any passenger or like quantity of freight of the same class over a greater distance on the same railroad, it should be deemed guilty of unjust discrimination, and be liable to a specified penalty. The specific discrimination complained of was a greater charge per car-load from Gilman to New York than from Peoria to New York, on the same class of freight—Gilman being nearer to New York than Peoria,

---

[1] Wabash, etc., R. R. Co. *vs.* Illinois, 118 U. S., 557. (Prior to Interstate Commerce Act.)

and the portion of the railroad between Gilman and Peoria being wholly within the State. The Illinois court held that the amount of the charge in each instance for the distance traversed through the State was proportioned to the amount charged for the whole distance to New York, and hence that the law of the State forbidding a greater charge for the less distance was violated within its own limits.

The sole question before the Supreme Court was the validity of the Illinois law, in the absence of Congressional legislation covering the subject [1]; and upon this question the members of the court were divided, both as to the principles underlying it and as to the effect of previous decisions, as precedents in point. The Chief-Justice and Justices Bradley and Gray were of opinion that the Illinois law was valid both upon principle and precedent. Justice Bradley, delivering the opinion of the minority, made an exceedingly clear and forcible argument in vindication of their views, based upon the power of the State over its own highways. And he declared that the very point in question had already been decided in one of the Granger cases.[2] An examination of these cases alone certainly seems to sustain Judge Bradley's opinion, and the majority of the court admit them to be susceptible of his construction. But Justice Miller, speaking for the majority of the court, after reviewing a number of cases on the

---

[1] This was before the passage of the Interstate Act of Congress.
[2] Peik *vs.* Railroad Co., 94 U. S., 164.

subject, said: "We must, therefore, hold that it is not, and never has been, the deliberate opinion of a majority of this court that a statute of a State, which attempts to regulate the fares and charges by railroad companies within its limits, for a transportation which constitutes a part of commerce among the States, is a valid law. . . . Of the justice or propriety of the principle which lies at the foundation of this statute, it is not the province of this court to speak. As restricted to a transportation which begins and ends within the limits of the State, it may be very just and equitable, and it certainly is the province of the State legislature to determine that question ; but when it is attempted to apply to transportation through an entire series of States a principle of this kind, and each one of the States shall attempt to establish its own rates of transportation, its own methods to prevent discrimination in rates, or to permit it, the deleterious influence upon the freedom of commerce among the States, and upon the transit of goods through those States, cannot be overestimated. That this species of regulation is one which must be, if established at all, of a general and national character, and cannot be safely and wisely remitted to local rules and regulations, we think is clear from what has already been said. And if it be a regulation of commerce, as we think we have demonstrated it is, and as the Illinois court concedes it to be, it must be of that national character ; and the regulation can only appropriately exist by general rules and principles, which demand that it should be done by the Congress of the United States, under the commerce clause of the Constitution."

Inasmuch, however, as interstate commerce is carried on principally by means of through-traffic arrangements between the railroad corporations of different States, the question arises whether a State may prevent the railroad companies of other States from making contracts with its own corporations for the mutual interchange of traffic "among the States," or may impose conditions upon such contracts; or whether, on the other hand, Congress can compel railroad corporations of different States to make such through-traffic arrangements with each other, against the expressed policy of one or more of the States.

The general rule as to the power of the States in respect to corporations of other States is that "they may exclude the foreign corporation entirely, they may restrict its business to particular localities, or they may exact such security for the performance of its contracts with its citizens as in their judgment will best promote the public interests." And this is because a "corporation, being the mere creature of local law, can have no legal existence beyond the limits of the sovereignty where created. The recognition of its existence, even by other States, and the enforcement of its contracts made therein, depend purely upon the comity of those States,—a comity which is never extended where the existence of the corporation, or the exercise of its powers are prejudicial to their interests or repugnant to their policy."[1] The terms of this rule are certainly broad enough to include the right of a State to exclude railroad companies of other States from doing any business, or making any contract to be performed within its limits, or to impose on such contracts such terms and conditions as it may deem expedient.

But this principle was announced in a case where the particular corporation under discussion was not engaged in commerce among the States.

And it has since been decided that the doctrine laid down in that case, that no State is bound to recognize within its limits the contracts, or even the existence, of a foreign corporation, is subordinate, and must yield to the paramount right of Congress to regulate commerce among the States. And Congress may not only authorize the admission of foreign corporations into a State, for the purpose of engaging in interstate commerce, against the consent of the State,[2] but the States cannot, even where Congress has not acted, exclude foreign corporations from engaging in such commerce within their limits.[3]

It being established that a foreign corporation may enter into a State, for the purpose of engaging therein in commerce among the States, even against the State's consent, it seems to follow that no State can prevent its own railroad corporations from entering into any contract

---

[1] Paul *vs.* Virginia, 8 Wall, 181.

[2] Pensacola Tel. Co. *vs.* W. U. Tel. Co., 96 U. S., 1.

[3] Cooper Mfg. Co. *vs.* Ferguson, 113 U. S., 726 ; Pickard *vs.* Car Co., 117 U. S., p. 34.

or traffic arrangement, *fairly within the scope of its powers*, with any foreign corporation, for the purpose of engaging in such commerce.

And, for the same reason, Congress may compel corporations of different States, engaged in interstate commerce, to make such traffic arrangements among themselves for carrying on such commerce *as are fairly within the scope of their powers*, to the same extent that it can compel natural persons so engaged to do so.

But whether a domestic corporation of a State can enter into a contract clearly *ultra vires*, and beyond the scope of its powers, with a foreign corporation, for the purpose of enabling the latter to engage in interstate commerce in the State of the domestic corporation, is a more difficult question. For example, a railroad corporation cannot lease or alien any franchise, or any property necessary to perform its duties and obligations to the State without legislative authority from that State. Such a lease would be *ultra vires* and void.[1]

The same is true of a consolidation of two or more railroad companies without legislative authority.[2] And the reason for this "is that where a corporation like a railroad company has granted to it a charter, intended in large measure to be exercised for the public good, the due performance of those functions being the consideration of the public grant, any contract which disables the

---

[1] Thompson *vs.* Railroad Co., 101 U. S., 71.
[2] Clearwater *vs.* Meredith, 1 Wall, p, 39.

corporation from performing those functions, which undertakes without the consent of the State to transfer to others the rights and powers conferred by the charter, and to relieve the grantees of the burden which it imposes, is a violation of the contract with the State, and is void as against public policy." The validity of railroad leases and consolidations has not been considered by the Supreme Court with reference to the effect on interstate commerce. But a lease or consolidation, being a total surrender of the functions of the corporation, and a violation of its contract with the State, is a very different thing from a mere traffic contract with another company, under which the corporation still retains the power to discharge all its duties and all the public objects of its creation. It by no means follows, therefore, even if a State cannot prevent its railroad corporations from entering into interstate traffic arrangements with railroad companies of other States, that leases or consolidations of its railroads with those of other States, or those chartered by Congress, are valid without its consent. Congress has, it is true, authorized the consolidation of a railroad chartered by it, with a road chartered by a State, but the constitutionality of the act has been questioned by the State authorities, and has not been passed on by the Supreme Court.[1]

One of the principal evils connected with the railroad

---

[1] See Ames *vs.* Kansas, 111 U. S., p. 449. See also Pacific R. R. Removal cases, 115 U. S., p. 16.

transportation system of the present day, is the excessively low rates on competitive traffic as compared with "local" or non-competitive traffic.

The evil here alluded to does not, however, seem to have been apprehended in the earlier days of railroad construction and transportation, and it is only in recent years that public attention has been closely attracted to it.

The danger formerly apprehended was that the railroad companies, being chartered by the States, might by their charges and methods of management, and by combinations to prevent competition among themselves, impede the free interchange of commerce among the States. It was apparently conceded without question that the railroads might fix their own rates, even on interstate transportation, subject only to such limitations as the States which chartered them might impose. And the idea seems to have prevailed that the means of preventing or removing obstructions to commerce arising in this way, would be the construction, under Federal authority, of competing lines of interstate commuincation.[1] Within the last decade, public attention has been called to the fact that discrimination, or relative extortion, and not usually actual extortion, is the crying evil of railway transportation. The legislative and the judicial mind of the country, too, have been coming to the conclusion that private competition cannot be relied on as a remedy for these evils, and

---

[1] See Railroad Co. *vs.* Maryland, 21 Wall, 473.

that governmental regulation of railways is both necessary and admissible.

The belief, too, has become current, and has finally resulted in legislation, that Congress can exercise its powers of regulating interstate commerce, upon the various State agencies engaged therein, without resorting to the doubtful and, for the most part, untried expedient of constructing competing lines under Federal authority. The power of Congress in the regulation of commerce among the States carried on by railroads has not yet been judicially defined with any degree of accuracy. But that railroads, within proper limits, are subject to that power, admits of no doubt.[1] In considering the powers of the Federal legislature over the prices and the modes of interstate commerce by railroad, and in the regulation of such commerce generally, it will aid in simplifying the discussion to bear in mind separately the respective functions of the carrier on the road, and those of the road itself, as a public highway for commerce.

The carrier, whether an individual or a corporation, whether by rail or turnpike, who holds himself out as such, is bound by the nature of his business to carry all classes of property which he assumes to carry, for all persons, without distinction or discrimination, regardless of the original starting-point or ultimate destination of the shipment. He is as much bound to carry persons or property whose transit begins in one State and is destined

---

[1] See Wabash, etc., R. R. Co. *vs.* Illinois, *ante*.

to end in another, as he is to carry those whose transit begins and ends in the same State. In assuming these obligations, the carrier does so—in legal contemplation at least—with knowledge of the public supervision and control which may be exercised over his business. This control proceeds from State authority or from Federal authority, according as the property transported belongs to domestic commerce or to interstate commerce. In undertaking voluntarily the business of a common carrier, and as such transporting persons and property *en route* from State to State, he by his own act submits himself to the regulative powers of Congress over commerce among the States. The powers of Congress over the railroad itself as a public highway are also derived from the fact that the road is an instrumentality of commerce among the States or with foreign nations, and such it must necessarily be to justify the exercise of Federal control over it. But where a railroad is built between such points as to manifest the intention of its owners, and of the State which authorizes its construction, to devote it to the transportation of commerce over which Congress has control, the intention to submit the road itself to the regulation of Congress, in respect of such commerce, is necessarily to be inferred. And Congress may, if it sees fit, impose regulations as to the mode of use of the road in carrying interstate traffic, which are repugnant to special and exclusive privileges that may have been conferred on its owners by the State. For the State cannot grant special privileges, except as to matters within its own power and control.

If it be objected that the road itself is a public agency created by the State—a State highway,—and therefore cannot be interfered with by Congress, the premises may be admitted, but the conclusion must be denied. The road is indeed a public agency, established by the State for the purpose of engaging in commerce ; but the commerce is both domestic and interstate in its character—the one being subject to State, the other to Federal regulation. And analogous examples are at hand where a State agency, exercising, under State authority, functions which are partially subject to Federal control, has actually been subjected to Federal regulation. Thus it frequently happens that elections for members of Congress and for State officers are held at the same time and place, and are presided over by State officers of election. The Constitution gives Congress the power to alter regulations which may be prescribed by any State as to the time, place, and manner of electing representatives to Congress. In pursuance of this power Congress has provided that any officer of an election at which a representative in Congress is voted for, whether such officer be acting under *State* or Federal authority, who neglects or refuses to perform any duty required of him in respect to such election, *by any law of the United States*, shall be liable to prescribed penalties. This is clearly a case of Federal regulation of an agency created by a State for the discharge of duties, some of which are subject to State supervision alone, and others to Federal supervision and control. And this legislation of Congress has been held to be valid and constitutional by the Supreme Court of the United States.[1] The authority of Congress over State officers presiding over congressional elections is derived from the constitutional grant of power to regulate the manner of holding such elections. Its power to regulate railroads built under State authority, over which interstate commerce is carried on, is as clearly inferrible from the constitutional grant of power to regulate such commerce. In neither case can the Federal power of regulation be carried so far as to impair substantially the domestic functions, peculiarly under the control of the State itself, which the State agency was intended to perform.

In both cases it may be exercised in whatever manner may be "necessary and proper," or "appropriate and plainly adapted," for the execution of the powers expressly conferred on Congress by the Constitution. A railway commission appears to be as "appropriate and plainly adapted" to the execution of the commercial power, as a National Bank of circulation was held to be, for the execution of other powers expressly conferred on Congress.[2] The consideration of railroads and railroad companies as State agencies for the performance of a proper function of the State—that is, furnishing highways

---

[1] *Ex parte* Siebold, 100 U. S., p. 371.
[2] McCulloch *vs.* Maryland, 4 Wheaton, 316.

for transportation—suggests one of the limitations of Federal control over the railroad system. Not only is Congress without authority to interfere directly with the domestic commerce of a State; but it cannot, it would seem, rightfully exercise any control over the railroads, or the companies which operate them, which will indirectly impair their responsibility to the State, or their capacity to discharge those domestic duties whose due performance was the consideration of their charters. For this reason it has been above suggested that Congress cannot authorize the consolidation or leasing of railroads built under State authority. It must be borne in mind that railroads are public highways, and though built by private parties, " the function performed is that of the State."[1] And so far as commerce confined within the State is concerned, it is a function necessary to its welfare and beyond the control of any extraneous authority. " The Federal Constitution ought not to be so construed as to impair, much less destroy, any thing that is essential to the efficient existence " of the State.[2]

It is true that the power of Congress has been judicially sustained, to tax out of existence Banks of Circulation chartered by the States,[3] although two judges dissented on the ground that the banks were public agencies of the States. But the decision in the case was put upon the ground that Congress had *exclusive* power over the

---

[1] Olcott *vs.* Supervisors, *ante.*
[2] Case of State tax on railroad gross receipts, 15 Wall, 284.
[3] Veazie Bank *vs.* Fenno, 8 Wall, 533.

currency of the whole country; and this is a very different thing from its commercial power, which is limited to commerce *among* the States, etc., and cannot affect commerce *within* a State. Over the latter, and the agencies created to carry it on, the powers of the State are as exclusive as those of Congress over interstate commerce.

And if Congress cannot authorize consolidations and leases of State railroads, neither can it prevent them. The ownership and title to property within the limits of a State is not a matter for Federal interference. Congress may regulate the price of the use, and the mode of use, and contracts in relation to the use of railroads, so far as they directly affect commerce among the States. Thus Congress may properly prohibit pooling contracts, which provide for a division of the traffic itself among diferent roads. Such a contract directly affects commerce.

But whether Congress can prohibit contracts which provide merely for a division of earnings among railroad companies has been questioned. On the one hand, it may be said that such contracts are made to prevent competition among the companies, in the transportation of traffic among the States, and that they are therefore obstructions to commerce among the States which Congress may constitutionally forbid. On the other hand, it has been decided that although a tax imposed by a State on the *transportation* of interstate traffic by railroad is void, as being a regulation of interstate commerce,[1] yet a

---

[1] Case of State freight tax, 15 Wall, 232.

State tax on the *earnings* of a railroad derived from such traffic is not a regulation of commerce, and is valid.[1]

If, then, a State can validly interfere with the earnings of a railroad from interstate traffic, because such interference is *not* a regulation of commerce among the States, it is difficult to see how the interference of Congress with the disposition the companies choose to make of their earnings can be sustained on the ground that it *is* a regulation of commerce among the States. The authority of the case last referred to has, however, been greatly weakened by a more recent decision,[2] and it can scarcely be doubted that the power of Congress to prohibit a division of earnings, or a "money pool" in interstate traffic, would at this day be judicially sustained.

The query has also been made whether Congress has power to sanction or legalize the general principle of pooling among railroads engaged in commerce among the States, or to legalize agreements between different companies to maintain rates on competitive interstate traffic.

Conceding that Congress may in proper cases regulate contracts between carrier and shipper, which are a necessary part of commerce itself, it is nevertheless suggested that pooling agreements are entirely different from the latter class of contracts; that they are not any part of commerce, and that therefore Congress cannot prohibit them, or legalize them, or otherwise regulate them. On

---

[1] Case of tax on railroad receipts. *Id.*, 284.
[2] P. & S. Steamship Co. *vs.* Pennsylvania, 122 U. S., 326.

the other hand, many persons are of opinion that these pooling agreements, under proper restrictions, are beneficial to commerce, in preventing unjust discriminations, and instability and fluctuations in the charges of railroad companies; and it is unquestionable that they have exercised a very decided influence upon commerce by rail. Their legalization and regulation, as well as their prohibition, as applied to interstate commerce, seems to be clearly within the authority of Congress. But whatever may be the power of Congress over pooling agreements, the futility of prohibiting pooling by act of Congress is plain, wherever the States think proper to permit consolidations of competing lines.

The national government, as well as the several States, is also limited in its control and regulation of railways, by the consideration of the private-property rights of their owners. "The United States cannot, any more than a State, interfere with private rights, except for legitimate governmental purposes. They are not included within the constitutional prohibition which prevents the State from passing laws impairing the obligation of contracts, but equally with the States they are prohibited from depriving persons or corporations of property without due process of law."[1] The limitations upon legislative power growing out of these considerations have already been examined. The exclusive powers of the States over their domestic commerce, and of Congress over interstate

---

[1] See Sinking Fund cases, 99 U. S., 718.

commerce, and the fact that the revenues of the railways are derived from both these sources, makes the proper application of this limitation very difficult, unless there shall be harmonious action on the subject between the Federal and State authorities.

One of the most important considerations involved in the question of the reasonableness of railroad charges, is that of the earnings of the companies. Many companies operate lines extending through several States. In each of these States they do a large business which is entirely confined within State limits; and they also do a large interstate business. The earnings, of course, are derived from the aggregate of the traffic within each State and between the States. Each sovereignty has regulative powers within its sphere, but the justice or expediency of the regulation may depend upon conditions which are under the control of a different sovereignty, and some concert of action between them would appear to be essential to success. The laws of one State, limiting railroad charges within its jurisdiction, may possibly operate indirectly to make charges on the same road higher in other States, or on interstate traffic. A company may endeavor to compensate for a diminution of revenues sustained by the legislation of one State, by increased charges on traffic over which that State has no control. Under these circumstances, questions of great delicacy may be presented, for whose final solution the Federal courts must be appealed to.

There is at least one important limitation on the power

of a State over its railroad corporations in their domestic commerce, which does not apply to the powers of Congress over them in their interstate commerce. This is the limitation which is frequently imposed by a contract between a State and a railroad company contained in its charter. These contracts usually relate to the rates which the companies may charge, and to the exclusive right of transportation over their roads; although they may of course relate to other subjects. But the State cannot surrender or relinquish by contract any rights but its own, or confer any greater powers than itself possesses. And Congress is therefore not at all hindered by any State charter from reducing or fixing railroad charges on interstate traffic below the tariff of charges authorized by the State, even though the latter has pledged itself not to reduce the tariffs. Nor, it would seem, can a railroad company claim the exclusive right of transporting interstate traffic over its road,—although by its charter from the State it enjoys that exclusive right,—where Congress prescribes a different mode of use. This would not be a requirement which, if reasonably applied (for instance, to compel a free interchange of traffic), would impair the authority of the State over its railroads, or the capacity of the latter for the transportation of commerce within the State.

THE ECONOMIC ASPECTS OF THE QUESTION.

CHAPTER V.

Extortion—Discriminations of Various Kinds—Relations of Railroads to Each Other and to Water Routes—Results thereof—Competition and Monopoly—Relative Charges for Long and Short Distances—Illustrations and Effects thereof—Discussion of the Long- and Short-Haul Question—Under What Circumstances and Conditions a Greater Charge for a Shorter Haul Justifiable—Illustrations and Analogies.

HAVING examined somewhat in detail the authority of the legislatures, both State and National, over railroad transportation, as well as the constitutional limitations upon legislative powers, it is proper to give some account of certain railroad methods and practices against which legislation has been invoked. No extended discussion of the subject, however, will be entered upon, but only a few illustrations given from the voluminous testimony which has been adduced concerning it. And here it is to be observed that the leading object had in view in fixing railway charges, is always to produce the largest net earnings from the operation of the road. This is an irresistible deduction from the first principles of human nature. All men will naturally seek to make the most of their own, and should proprietary rights in this respect conflict with public rights, the former will surely have the preference at the hands of the management. And yet these charges are perhaps in no case of that entirely arbitrary character which has sometimes been predicated of them. They are in the first place limited by the general doctrine of the common law, that they must be reasonable; though the difficulties to be encountered in seeking relief from real or supposed extortion under this general principle are so great as to make it of little value. The direct limitation imposed by the existence of competition is frequent and striking, but it is by no means sufficiently pervasive to make its influence of universal benefit; and indeed it has sometimes operated to produce any thing but beneficial results. In the third place, where neither the reasonableness of the charge, from the shipper's standpoint, nor the necessity of meeting competition, affects the action of the railway management in fixing rates, there are other considerations which will always exert an influence (though sometimes an inadequate one) to modify the purely arbitary character of charges. These considerations, when duly weighed and given their proper influence by a management seeking merely to increase net revenues, operate to place the rate on any given commodity at such a figure as that the product of the rate and the quantity of the shipment, minus the expense of the carriage, will be a maximum.

Low rates of transportation stimulate production and increase shipments, and there must evidently be some point between an excessively high and an excessively low charge, where the product of the rate and the volume of traffic will be a maximum. This point in practice can, of course, only be approximately ascertained, and that only by experiment. Up to that point decrease of rates increases gross earnings; while the increase of operating expenses is by no means in proportion to increase of traffic. Hence mere considerations of profit to the company may undoubtedly influence a wise management to reduce rates at non-competitive points. But this effect of lowering railway charges does not always seem to be clearly apprehended by those having control of such matters; and after all, as the underlying principle of this last limitation is a purely selfish one with the railway, and intended only to increase its revenues, it must be conceded that charges, unless influenced by competition, are to a very large extent arbitrary. Such at all events they are wellnigh universally believed to be—the shipper having no immediate voice in fixing them,—and from this belief great dissatisfaction with railway methods, more or less well founded, has arisen.

Charges of injustice in the operation of railways relate chiefly to extortion and unjust discrimination. It has already been suggested that extortion in a general sense, as distinguished from discrimination, may be defined as imposing on the public such classifications and schedules of rates as will in the aggregate swell the net earnings of the road beyond a reasonable compensation on the just value of the property.

What the just value of railroad property is, is not always by any means an easy matter to determine. It is not necessarily what similar property could be built or bought for at the time of the valuation. To estimate it on that consideration alone would frequently do gross injustice to security holders. The prices of labor and material may have fallen greatly between the time of construction and the time of valuation, and to throw the whole loss thus sustained on security holders would be manifestly unjust. Still this consideration should certainly enter into the estimate of just value. Other elements of course enter into the estimate, such as the actual *bona fide* original cost, the amount of "water" in securities, etc.[1] No satisfactory basis for determining the just value of railroad property, especially when the franchises are considered, has been, or in the nature of things probably can be, established. From the purely proprietary standpoint the value should be estimated only by earning capacity. Even this is largely dependent upon changing circumstances, such as crop prospects, or the volume of traffic as affected by the general financial condition of the country, and to an even greater extent per-

---

[1] For views of this question from very different standpoints see testimony of Fink and Thurber before Senate Committee on Labor and Capital, vol. ii., pp. 463 to 522, and 743 to 784.

haps upon the personal characteristics of the managing officials. The policy pursued by a directory—whether conservative and economical, or aggressive and daring—is a great factor in the determination of the current value of the property. Various methods of approximating the value have been suggested. One is by averaging the net earnings for a series of years, and computing the amount of capital required to produce annually the amount of the average annual net earnings at a fair rate of interest; another is to ascertain the value of the entire bonded debt and stock of the company, at the ruling market prices; and a third is that by appraisement. The method of valuation by appraisement must usually be the merest guesswork, unless the appraisement is to some extent based upon the other methods suggested, *i. e.*, the average net earnings and the market value of securities. But to adopt them as a basis of value seems to be a concession of the claim that the value is limited only by earning capacity—a claim that may sometimes be highly prejudicial to the public welfare.[1] How far the companies are entitled to the "unearned increment" of value arising from the general increase in the wealth and population of the country, is a very difficult question. Many thousands of miles of railway have been built into the wilderness, without any hope or prospect of immediate

---

[1] For discussions of this question of the *value* of railway property, see Third Semi-annual Report of Railway Commission of Georgia, p. 37, Report of Interstate Commerce Committee, 1888, p. 64; and *R. R. Gazette*, 1888, p. 743.

return upon investment. The future development of the country, which the railroad must itself create, can alone bring profit to the enterprise. Of the fruits of such development, those whose sagacity and whose capital have largely contributed to produce it, are surely entitled to a liberal share. Even in populous commercial communities, where railroad earnings are from the start reasonably remunerative, the existence of the railway is frequently a prime cause of further commercial development and increase of wealth. To deny to the railway companies any share in this increase, would seem to savor strongly of the doctrines of Henry George. Yet this is what many persons seem to think should be done. On the other hand, to permit them to appropriate to themselves in the shape of earnings the utmost amount an enormous traffic will yield, is to overlook the fact that railroads are public highways.[1] The general public are entitled to share the benefits in the shape of reduced transportation charges. No less an authority than Mr. Charles F. Adams, Jr., has asserted that a railroad company should not even apply its earnings to new construction, but that fresh capital should be invested for that purpose ; and where the earnings more than suffice to pay operating expenses, debts, and reasonable dividends on stock, rates should be reduced and the public relieved of its burdens.[2]

---

[1] For Mr. Jay Gould's views, see vol. i. of testimony before Senate Committee on Labor and Capital, p. 1074.
[2] Report Mass. R. R. Commission, 1875, pp. 12, 13.

There are instances where earnings have been applied to new construction, and additional stock issued to represent it; and there are others where, though earnings have been applied to new construction, no new stock was issued therefor.

But modern railroad enterprises are usually sufficiently capitalized in their inception to render future stock watering unnecessary, and the application of earnings to new construction impossible. It is generally believed, and is perhaps in large measure true, that railroads nowadays are built entirely with the proceeds of mortgage bonds—not infrequently sold at a heavy discount,—and that the capital stock does not really represent money paid towards the construction of the work. It is notorious, too, that where railway property is bought in at foreclosure sales, the amount of stock and bonds issued against the property by the purchasers is vastly in excess of the purchase price. It does not necessarily follow that the new capitalization is in excess of the just value of the property; though perhaps in most cases it is so. Nor is it likely that excessive capitalization increases transportation rates, for these are, under all circumstances, adjusted with the view of securing the largest amount of net earnings.

But it is highly probable that the effort to pay interest and dividends on an excessive capitalization frequently causes a diversion of earnings from the proper maintenance and repairs of works and property, and is responsible for many calamitous railroad accidents. Without undertaking to say how the just value of railroad property should be ascertained—except that a liberal estimate should be made in favor of the owners of the property,—it still sufficiently appears that it may be a very different thing from the capitalized value. And the discussion, in previous chapters, of the legal relations between the railways and the public, clearly shows that the determination of the just value and reasonable net earnings of railway property belongs to the public; just as the valuation of lands, or other private property to be taken for public use, is made by public assessors. The valuation must, of course, be made " by due process of law," and, as has already been shown, must ultimately be judicially ascertained, in case of disagreement between the owners and the representatives of the public.

The earning capacity of different roads, and the average charges necessary to be imposed upon the public in order to earn a reasonable net return on the just value of the property, varies very greatly. Yet there is a singularly strong propensity in people—even intelligent people—to overlook this very evident truth, and to set up as a standard of reasonable charges upon one line, those for similar services upon another, whose traffic conditions may be totally different. This propensity is indeed but part of a larger fact, which constitutes one of the chief perplexities in dealing with complaints against railroad companies. This is that the public is apt to regard the entire railroad system of the country as a unit in respect of the capacity and responsibility of the many different roads composing it. Such an idea is, of course, entirely fallacious. It is safe to say, perhaps (though there are certainly exceptions to the assertion), that most railroad companies, whatsoever the wishes or the efforts of the management may be, do not make on the entire operation of their property an excessive net return upon its just value. Very inconsistent demands are often made upon railway managements,—for the lowest traffic charges on the one hand, and on the other for the highest efficiency in the public service, and the most approved appliances for speed, comfort, and safety. Enforced diminution of revenues is very apt to result in decreased efficiency of service, and probably in impairment of the safety and general condition of the property.

The number of trains per day may be reduced, and travel greatly inconvenienced. Scarcity of funds may be alleged as a reason for not introducing new inventions for the promotion of safety. Possibly bridges and other structures will not receive the attention which the safety and accommodation of traffic and travel demand. Where the companies do their full duty to the public in maintaining their facilities and property in the highest possible condition of efficiency, their net earnings will not usually be in excess of what they are entitled to. This being the case, the question of what rate on any particular commodity or charge for any particular service is extortionate, or what is reasonable, must evidently be a relative one.

It would manifestly be impossible to predicate of the charge for any particular service that it is unreasonable or the reverse, without a close examination of the entire traffic and field of operations of the road. It would be necessary to consider not only the value of the property and its physical characteristics, but the quantity and the different kinds of traffic transported by it, its situation with reference to competitive routes, both generally and at special points, and in general all the complicated conditions which influence railroad rate-makers in fixing charges.

The principal problem to solve seems to be how to fix charges to produce a fair income, without unjustly discriminating between places, persons, and kinds of traffic; to so adjust rates as to impose as equitably as possible upon various interests and various localities and various shippers, the burden of the necessary aggregate of charges to cover all expenses. The best efforts have not entirely succeeded in the accomplishment of this difficult task. Discrimination, therefore, is a much more prolific source of complaint than actual extortion, especially in the transportation of freights. And as the passenger traffic is comparatively of minor importance, and less the subject of complaint, the following illustrations and observations will be confined principally to freight transportation.

Discriminations may be against or in favor of particular species of traffic or commodities, against or in favor of particular individuals, or against or in favor of certain localities. To understand, in the first place, how these discriminations come to exist, and in the second place, to understand how far they constitute real evils, and how far imaginary evils only,—and if real, how far they are attributable to the intentional policy of the railroads, and how far to circumstances beyond their control or that of legislation,—the geography of the railroad system must be studied : that is, the extent of the various lines of railway, and their location with reference to one another and to water routes, as well as to points of production, manufacture, exportation, and consumption. A comprehensive examination of the geography of the whole railroad system of the United States would of course be impracticable here. But there are certain groups of railroad lines which form quite distinct systems within themselves, the leading features and effects of which may be easily understood. Of these systems what are called the " Trunk Lines," with their connections, constitute the most important, and have presented in their operation and management perhaps all the abuses of railroad transportation, while at the same time illustrating the splendid public services of the railroads in the development of the country. The trunk-line system embraces the lines of railroads connecting the upper Mississippi valley with the Atlantic seaboard, or, as more usually and definitely understood, such of those lines as lie east of the Mississippi, and north of the Ohio and Potomac rivers. The eastern termini of the trunk lines are at Boston, New York, Philadelphia, and Baltimore. The objective point of all of them in the west is Chicago,—the great entrepot of the products of the west and northwest on their way east —and with it all of them have connections more of less direct, by routes more or less circuitous. The trunk lines proper embrace at present the Grand Trunk of Canada, the New York Central, the West Shore, the Erie, the Delaware, Lackawanna, & Western, the Pennsylvania, and the Baltimore & Ohio railroads. There is competition between all these lines in transportation from Chicago and other railroad centres in the west, to the seaboard. There is also competition at some points of railway intersection between the west and the seaboard. But at the vast majority of points on the trunk lines and their connecting (or affiliating) roads, the respective roads have an absolute monopoly of transportation.

One of the most important factors in the trunk line situation lies outside of the railroads themselves. This is the water route from Chicago to the Atlantic, furnished by the Great Lakes, the Erie Canal, and the Hudson River.

The influence of water routes in controlling the rates of railways has been explained by some of the highest authorities on transportation in the country. In the report of the Hepburn Committee (p. 39), it is said : " While the committee made no attempt to investigate the relations of the railroads to the canal, and sought to lessen their labors by avoiding this question, the canal, like Banquo's ghost, would not down, but we were compelled to meet it at every point and turn of the investigation. The cost of water transportation from Chicago to New York is the base line upon which rates are determined and fixed, throughout the country. The rates by agreement of the principal railroads of the country are made a certain percentage of the Chicago rate (Testimony, pp. 3001, '2, '3, '4). Thus, Cincinnati is 87 per cent. of the Chicago rate, St. Louis 116 per cent., Kansas City 146 per cent., Louisville 96 per cent., Cleveland $73\frac{1}{2}$ per cent., etc. There remains for the railroads to do this additional act of justice, and see that rates from points in the State of New York, to the city of New York, are made a proper percentage of the Chicago rate." And Mr. Blanchard, one of the most eminent men in the railroad profession, says: "The rail charges from Chicago to New York, lasting through seven months or more in twelve, are as inflexibly controlled by the charges of the Lakes and St. Lawrence River, and the Erie Canal and the Hudson River, as the charges of one merchant in good standing and business, are regulated by those of another good merchant in the same general interests and business across the street."[1]

The far-reaching influence of water rates upon the rates of railways is fully explained in a letter from Albert Fink, commissioner of the associated trunk lines, to Senator Windom, then chairman of the committee of the United States Senate, on "Transportation Routes to the Sea-

---

[1] Testimony, Cullom Committee, p. 149.

board." He says: "When the rates are reduced between Chicago and New York, on account of the opening of the canal, the reduction applies not only from Chicago, but from all interior cities (St. Louis, Indianapolis, Cincinnati) to New York. If that were not the rule, the result would be that the roads—running say from St. Louis, Indianapolis, and Cincinnati, to Chicago—would carry the freight to Chicago, from which point low rail or water rates would take it to the East, and leave the direct railroad routes from these interior points to the seaboard without any business. Hence, whenever rates are reduced on account of the opening of navigation from Chicago and the Lake ports, the same reduction is made from all interior cities not only to New York, where the canal runs, but to Boston, Philadelphia, and Baltimore. Although the latter cities have no direct water communication with the West, yet they receive the benefit as far as low railroad rates are concerned, to the same extent as if a canal was actually running from the Lakes direct to those cities, because whenever rates from Chicago to New York are reduced, it becomes absolutely necessary to reduce correspondingly the rates from Chicago to Boston, Philadelphia, and Baltimore, otherwise these cities could do no business, as it would all go to New York. The reduction of the rates from Chicago and St. Louis to New York, Baltimore, etc., reduces the rates from Western points via New York, Baltimore, and ocean, to the Southern Atlantic ports. . . . The railroads running directly from Chicago and St. Louis, via Louisville, Nashville, and Chattanooga, to the same points, are obliged to follow the reductions made via the rail and ocean routes. . . . The same is true in relation to the West-bound traffic. . . . There need be no fear that extortionate rates will be charged by railroad companies; on the contrary, the fear is that water competition will be so effective as to prevent railroads from securing paying rates."[1] It is just here that the trouble arises; that is, from the effectiveness of water competition in keeping down the rates of railways at competing points, to figures which, if everywhere maintained, would reduce the revenues of the roads in many cases below what they are entitled to earn. The result of the competition existing between the railroads themselves and the railroads and the canal, so long as fairly maintained, is, of course, to prevent extortionately high charges between competing points; that is to say—speaking generally of the trunk-line system—between the west and the seaboard. And between different important points in the west and tide-water on the east rates are adjusted with some reference at least to the length of the haul. But the closing sentence of the above quotation from the Hepburn Committee's report suggests the existence of a different state of things at non-competitive points,

---

[1] See Reports on Internal Commerce of U. S. for 1885, p. 433; also for 1886, part II., pp. 343, 344. For the practical method of adjusting rates see testimony before Interstate Commerce Commission at Atlanta, etc., vol. i., Repts.

and intimates the concurrence of its authors in the popular opinion that transportation charges should bear a somewhat uniform ratio to distance. Examination shows this opinion to be incorrect. Any attempt to establish rates over long and short hauls even upon the same line of road, strictly in proportion to distance, must always be impracticable. This is partly due to the fact that several elements of cost, especially the terminal expenses, are the same in either case, so that the actual cost of service is greater in proportion to distance upon the short haul, than upon the long. But a more potent reason is that rates fixed strictly in proportion to length of haul would be so high as to prohibit the transportation of most commodities between widely separated points. All revenue from long-distance traffic would thereby be cut off, whereas by taking it at lower rates the revenues are increased. It is analogous to fixing a tariff on imported goods, which may be so high on any given article as to prohibit its importation, and thereby diminish revenues, which a lower rate of duty would increase.[1] This argument for low long-distance rates, it is true, proceeds from considerations of the carriers' interest only; but the general public welfare equally demands the maintenance of this salutary principle of railroad transportation. For upon it is based the immense internal commerce of the country, whereby exchanges of products are effected between the most distant por-

---

[1] Hadley's " Railroad Transportation," p. 110.

tions of the Union, and all sections bound together by the strongest ties of mutual interest. By it the fields of production are enormously expanded; the values of lands remote from markets are enhanced; the price of every necessity of life is reduced; the surplus products of the interior—West and South,—amounting to hundreds of millions in value, are brought to the seaboard, to be ultimately laid down in the markets of Europe, and the balance of trade is preserved in favor of America. Undoubtedly the application of this principle has produced great hardships, especially to the agricultural interests of the Atlantic States; but the number of people benefited by this levelling process is vastly greater than the number who suffer from it, and it is quite vain for the latter to hope for the advantages they once enjoyed. Yet while the unfortunate results alluded to are in large measure inevitable, they have often been aggravated to an extent that cannot be justified. For the principle just considered cannot alone account for the exaggerated disproportion which frequently exists between charges on long and short hauls. In fact, not only are rates not fixed in proportion to the distance to and from competitive points, as compared with the rates and the distance to and from non-competitive points, but in some cases a higher absolute charge is made for the short haul where there is no competition, than for the longer haul where there is competition. The instances of this practice are too numerous to mention.

It seems to be part and parcel of the whole system of railroad management. The voluminous testimony which has been taken on the subject is replete with illustrations of it. It is one of the commonest forms of discrimination by railroads against localities. Two or three illustrations of the practice will suffice. For example, the town of Danville, Va., is reached by no railroad except that of the Richmond & Danville Company. The Richmond & Danville, however, has competitors for traffic between the south and southwest and the city of Richmond, Va. There being no competition at Danville, the railroad company was enabled to charge, and did charge, on a car-load of cattle from Newport, Tennessee, to Danville, $14 more than the current rate through Danville, 140 miles further, to Richmond. More was also charged on consignments of melons from Columbia, S. C., to Danville, than from the same point via Danville to Richmond.[1] The following instance is still more striking: "A merchant of Wilkesbarre, Pa., purchased a car-load of potatoes at Rochester, N. Y., and had the freight bill made for a delivery at Philadelphia, because the freight to Philadelphia was less than it was to Wilkesbarre, which is 143 miles nearer. He stopped the potatoes at Wilkesbarre, unloaded them, and paid the freight. A few days later he received a bill from the Lehigh Valley Railroad Company for $12 additional freight. If the potatoes had gone on to Philadel-

---

[1] See Interstate Com. Repts., vol. i., p. 707.

phia, he would have paid $48 freightage; as they stopped at Wilkesbarre, he had to pay $60; that is, $12 for not hauling the car-load 143 miles."[1] Railroad men sometimes attempt to justify this practice, on grounds of abstract right and justice, by various suggestions, such as the greater terminal expenses, in the case of the short haul, the loss incurred by leaving cars to stand idle at local stations, the inability (usually) to procure return loads there, etc. No doubt, there is force in these suggestions, but not enough by any means, as a general rule, to justify the disparity in charges in favor of the longer haul. And the argument as to the terminal expenses is offset by the fact (as asserted by Mr. Blanchard)[2] that the higher taxes, rents, and prices in large cities make the terminal expenses of railroads greater there than at the smaller towns and stations. And yet the large cities are termini of railways, centres of competition, and receive always the most favorable rates, which smaller intermediate places are usually unable to obtain.

General Devereux, president of one of the important western railroads, "speaking from an experience of over thirty-seven years of railroad service," said, in answer to the inquiry why a railroad company should charge more for a short than for a longer haul: "You cannot answer the question why it should charge more in any reasonable way."[3] The General, however, defended the practice,

---

[1] Test., Cullom Com., pp. 531, 532.   [2] *Id.*, pp. 153, 155.   [3] *Id.*, pp. 817, 837.

saying that the people who suffered from it probably enjoyed compensating advantages. " It may be from their beautiful location. Perhaps the beauty of the scenery or the merit of the town, or something of that sort, will account for it." It is frequently said, too, that so long as the local point is given rates reasonable in themselves there is no cause of complaint, simply because competitive points are given lower rates. And the rates at local points are demonstrated to be entirely reasonable, by comparison with the rates in existence before the advent of the railway. But the mere fact of a rate being high or low does not determine the welfare of a community or an individual. It is the question of relative rates. Thus to use the illustration given by Mr. Simon Sterne[1]: "The city of Santa Fé, in New Mexico, which was once a flourishing place, and the entrepot of the caravan trade, is in a condition of decadence. Its business is being removed to Las Vegas and Albuquerque; and yet the rates of transportation since a rail line has been built to it lately are much less than the rates which the ox-teams charged for going over the mountains into Santa Fé. But as the rates to Las Vegas and Albuquerque are still lower, they take the business, and Santa Fé is suffering decay. An intelligent witness who has made a special study of the subject, speaking of the effect of railroad discriminations upon the agricultural interests of Pennsylvania, says: " The losses to farmers at non-competitive points in the

---

[1] Testimony, Cullom Committee, p. 69.

State have been computed by a committee of the State Board of Agriculture at from six to eight per cent. of the annual product of their lands; and the census of 1880 showed that while the acreage of improved land had increased, and while the proportion of our non-agricultural population had increased in 1880, so that each farmer fed four other workers, as compared with three other workers in 1870, yet the value of our agricultural products had declined at the rate of $22,000,000 a year."[1]

The decline in the value of agricultural lands throughout the Atlantic States generally tells the same story.

An instance of the greater charge for the shorter haul, under peculiarly aggravating circumstances, was cited by Senator Wilson, of Iowa, in the debate on the Interstate Commerce bill.[2] It appears there was a large surplus of corn in western Iowa, and an almost total failure of the crop in the eastern part of the State, where it was greatly needed to feed the surplus stock; and yet the rates on corn from western Iowa and Omaha to points in eastern Iowa were higher than the rates from Omaha to Chicago. If the farmers of eastern Iowa had been given even the Chicago rate, it would, said Senator Wilson, have tided them over the exceptional period of depression and loss. As it was, the farmers had to sell their horses, cattle, and hogs in a depressed market at whatever prices they could get. Such are some of the results which have been proven to follow from discriminating in charges against non-competitive

---

[1] Test., Cullom Com., p. 531. [2] *Cong. Record*, 1886-7, pp. 329, 330.

points, as compared with the rates given competitive points where a longer haul is required. And one of the most astute and experienced railroad men in the country has been forced to confess that no good reason can be given for such discriminations.[1] But General Devereux must have meant this remark to apply only to those cases where discriminations are made arbitrarily, and not where the necessity of thus discriminating is forced upon the companies by circumstances which are beyond their control, and which acquit them of the charge of injustice to communities upon which the higher rates are imposed. How far discriminations of this character are arbitrarily imposed, merely to swell earnings beyond a fair return on the just value of the railroad property,—in which event they are of course unjust,—it is impossible to say, except after special examination of special cases of complaint. And it has already been shown that if railroad practices benefit the companies to the detriment of the community, it is the right and the duty of the State to interfere. But there is undoubtedly a large class of cases where an absolute prohibition to charge more for the short than for the long haul under any circumstances would work an injustice to the railroads without benefiting the community which is charged the higher rates.

The practice of charging more for the short than for the long haul—appearing as it does to reverse the natural advantages of geographical position—has been the

---

[1] See *ante*.

subject of so much popular animadversion that it is worth while to examine at some length the circumstances and conditions under which it appears to be justifiable. In doing this it will be assumed that a railroad company is justly entitled to charge such rates as will enable it to earn a reasonable net income on the just value of its property, *provided* this can be done without inflicting injury on any portion of the community it is intended to serve. This is surely a reasonable postulate. Discrimination which produces no injury cannot be considered unjust, and if it can be shown that discrimination may in certain cases be actually beneficial to the community apparently discriminated against, it should, instead of being denounced, be encouraged to the furthest limit of its beneficial operation. Justifiable discrimination in favor of the longer haul is the result of competition. It has been shown how rates by rail are affected by water rates. Where rail routes and water routes come in competition for the carriage of the same product, the rates by rail must be put nearly or quite as low as the rates by water, or else the water routes will take all the freight. And different routes (whether both rail, or one rail and one water) may be competitive, although they have only one common field or terminus for the collection or distribution of freights, while the other termini may be separated by hundreds or thousands of miles. It is by no means necessary that routes should be parallel to make them competitive. Thus the rail lines connecting upper Georgia with Chattanooga and Richmond respectively compete with each other in carrying the iron manufactures of those cities to their common territory in upper Georgia.[1] The lines connecting points in Alabama with Savannah and New Orleans respectively, compete in the carriage of cotton from their common territory to those markets.[2] The rail lines connecting the Southern lumber regions with the cities on the great lakes compete in the carriage of lumber with the lake vessels connecting those cities with the lumber regions of the Northwest.[3] The rail lines connecting the lime-kilns of Virginia with the South Atlantic cities[4] compete with coastwise vessels from Maine in the transportation of lime to those points. The rail lines connecting the pig-iron furnaces of the interior with the New England cities are frequently brought into competition with "tramp steamers" bringing in Scotch iron as ballast.[5] The water routes of the Mississippi River and its tributaries compete with the trunk lines and their tributaries in the transportation of the products of the Mississippi valley. That great territory is a common field or terminus of both systems of transportation, though the other terminus of the water routes is at New Orleans, and the other termini of the trunk lines are the cities of the North Atlantic coast. The other great water route from the West to the seaboard, to wit, that by the lakes and the Erie Canal, has

---

[1] See Rept. on Internal Commerce U. S. 1886, part 2, p. 334.
[2] See vol. i., Interstate Commerce Repts., p. 125, testimony of Ponder.
[3] *Id.*, p. 97.   [4] *Id.*, p. 106.   [5] *Id.*, p. 163, 164.

already been referred to as an essential factor in the establishment of railroad rates. The river route perhaps exerts a scarcely less potential influence.[1] Any considerable and permanent rise in railroad rates to and from the West would probably result in the diversion of the traffic to the water routes, thus cutting off the railroads from a considerable portion of their through traffic.

The same is true in respect to railroad rates between points on the North Atlantic coast and points on the South Atlantic and Gulf coasts, where competition exists between rail and water routes. It is equally true of the transcontinental lines connecting the Atlantic and Pacific oceans, and indeed wherever competition between rail and water routes exists. The mutual influence of the transportation routes of the world upon each other might indeed be shown to be far more pervasive than any thing here suggested would indicate. For it is not the commerce of one nation or continent alone, that determines the conditions of transportation within its limits, but that of the civilized world. The limited scope of this inquiry forbids entering upon so broad a field. Yet it sufficiently appears that at competitive points the rail charges must be so far reduced as to approximate the charges by water, or else the tonnage which will bear water transportation will go that way.

The question is thus presented, whether if the railroads are cut off from the " through " or competitive traffic,

---

[1] See Testimony, Cullom Committee, *passim*.

they can maintain their present net revenues without raising rates on local or non-competitive traffic. The question, in other words, is whether the reduction in expenses arising from the loss or abandonment of through traffic is less or more in actual amount than the reduction of the revenue.

It is by no means whether the earnings on through traffic are proportionately as great as the earnings on local or non-competitive traffic, but simply whether any earnings at all are derived from it, over and above the additional expense incurred in carrying the through traffic. It is easily demonstrable that this additional expense is trivial in amount compared with the immense increase in carrying capacity and in tonnage that may be secured by it; and where a large volume of through traffic can be obtained by a comparatively small additional outlay, it does undoubtedly, even at very low rates of transportation, add largely to the net earnings of the road. And by taking that competitive traffic even at those excessively low rates, the railroads, to the extent that any net revenue is derived from it, are enabled to reduce the rates on the local traffic, and still earn their reasonable net income.

If therefore it be true that water competition frequently limits railroad charges, it may be better for the local traffic that the competitive traffic should be taken at that limit, even though it be actually less than the local rate, for the shorter transportation; *provided*, always, the railways will make more, or *lose less*, by taking the competitive business than by refusing it,—that is will increase their net earnings. The reason which compels, and justifies, a railroad, in competition with water routes, to lower its rates at competitive points to figures, it may be, less than those charged for a shorter haul and less costly service, is simply that water transportation is, on the average, cheaper than rail transportation, and the railroad would not otherwise get the competitive business.

And this feature of railroad practice is justifiable only when the competitive business adds something—small though it may be—to net earnings.

Beyond this limit competition is certainly unjustifiable, and the competitive rate constitutes an unjust discrimination against the local traffic.

But it is easy to see that the average cost of transportation over one line of railway may as much exceed that over another which reaches the same competitive point or region, as the average cost of transportation over the latter exceeds the average cost of water carriage. The advantage of one rail line over another (competing line), in the average cost of carriage, may result from the lesser length of the line, lighter gradients, superiority of rolling stock, and condition of track, but above all from the greater volume of traffic which it enjoys.

A road thus fortunately circumstanced, passing through a rich and densely populated region, and receiving heavy freights at all points along its line, may well afford to haul at an average rate of say three fourths of a cent per ton per mile. And it is quite conceivable that such a road, even in competition with water, may so adjust its tariffs as never to charge more for the shorter than the longer haul, and still maintain its revenues at a figure affording an ample return on the just value of the property. But another rail line may have one terminus in a region or place, which affords the opportunity of competition with the road above described, while its other terminus may be reached only by a longer and steeper route, over an inferior track, through poor and sparsely settled communities which furnish but little freight. It may very likely be, and frequently is true, that such a road barely realizes net earnings sufficient to pay a meagre return upon the just value of the investment by charging an average rate of say one and a half cents per ton per mile. Such a road, to get any of the competitive business, must make its rates at least as low as its competitor. It may well do this and still make some small net earnings from the business. But if its local rates must be so reduced that the charge for the shorter shall never exceed that for the longer competitive haul, the net revenues will be so reduced as to afford a grossly inadequate return, if any, on the value of the property. To comply with a "long-and-short-haul" law forces a road in the predicament last described to adopt one of two alternatives. It must either lower its local rates to the level of competitive rates, which will almost certainly involve a loss of net earnings, or it must abandon the competitive traffic, in which latter event the question of net earnings will depend on whether the local or non-competitive traffic will bear any higher charge or not. If it will bear any higher charge, it will certainly be imposed, with the hope of producing net earnings sufficient to yield a reasonable income on investment. It is difficult to see how the adoption of this course by the railway, to make a reasonable income on its property, could be considered extortionate under such circumstances, but it would doubtless be a grievous burden to the local interests. To adopt the other alternative, and force the railways to lower their rates under such circumstances as have been supposed (and they frequently exist), is so unjust to the railway interests that it should never be forced upon them ; and, indeed, it would seem to be a violation of their constitutional rights. For be it observed that, in spite of the prohibition against charging more for the shorter than the longer haul, the more distant competitive points and regions still enjoy the benefit of the lower rates through the medium of the water routes and of the stronger railway lines, which are able to comply with the law, and at the same time maintain their revenues on a reasonably remunerative basis. The evil sought to be removed therefore remains unabated, and may very probably be aggravated by a long-and-short-haul law of general and imperative application.

The community or locality which has to pay the higher rates of course suffers grievously from the competition of the region which enjoys the advantages in the rates and facilities of transportation. It may even be compelled to abandon the industries which have long sustained it, and, at a great sacrifice of time and capital, to embark in others which are beyond the range of competitive influence. Thus the agriculture of the middle States of the Atlantic seaboard has inevitably declined under the pressure of western competition, and the railroads are generally regarded as the prime cause of the depression. Undoubtedly its cause is to be found, in large measure, in the cheap transportation by water routes and rail routes from the West to the seaboard. But the prohibition to charge less for the longer than the shorter haul will not help the situation of the eastern farmer, located on a weak line of railway, which is thereby compelled to abandon its competitive traffic, so long as the water routes and the strong rail routes comply with the law and still carry at the same low rates. Such a prohibition, resulting in the abandonment of the through traffic, may diminish the revenues of the road which serves the eastern farmer, but it will not enhance the prices of his products in the markets of the world, for they are governed by the cost of transportation over the cheapest routes by which the demand can be supplied. It is cheap transportation over other routes which puts him at a disadvantage, much more than the discrimination in favor of the longer haul by the line over which he ships. And one of the essentials to the justification of this discrimination is the existence of cheaper transportation over other routes. If the traffic from or to the competitive point will at all events be transported at a certain price, then a competing line is justified in taking it from or to that point at the same price, *provided its net earnings are thereby increased.* And the local shipper over the latter line is not prejudiced by its doing so.

The important question to the local shipper, and the question which public investigation should settle in such a case, is, whether the local rates may not be reduced, and still leave the net earnings sufficient to yield a fair return on the just value of the railroad property.

A large amount of the cheaper classes of freight is sometimes transported over long distances, at rates per ton per mile which are actually *less* than the *average cost* per ton per mile of the total transportation of freight. Paradoxical as it may appear, this may often be done, and still some net earnings be derived from the business. *How* it may be done may be understood when it is considered that the average cost of the total transportation consists in large part of items which vary very little, if any, with the volume of traffic, such as maintenance of way and other fixed charges; while the "additional cost" of any given amount of additional traffic consists almost solely of the expense immediately attendant upon its carriage—that is, the cost of conducting that particular item of transportation, which is but a small part of the entire operating expenses.

The reports annually made by railroad companies of their business operations, usually show the average rate per ton per mile received for the transportation of freight. In these reports the expenses of operating the road are also given, and are allotted part to passenger traffic and part to freight traffic. The operating expenses are further subdivided and distributed under the heads of "conducting transportation," of "motive power," of "maintenance of way," of "maintenance of cars," and of "general expenses." While this apportionment and distribution of expenses cannot be entirely accurate, it is sufficiently so for the purposes of the present reference.

An examination of these reports will show that the cost of "conducting transportation" allotted to freight traffic is frequently much less than one half the total operating expenses allotted to freight traffic.

The following illustrative figures are calculated from the report of a road which carries a large tonnage of coal over a distance exceeding four hundred miles, and also a considerable tonnage of cotton, corn, and other products from the Mississippi valley to the seaboard.[1]

There are doubtless cases where the road referred to charges a less rate than .382 cts. per ton-mile (or less than the average expense) for carrying freight, and yet it may make money by doing so.

---

[1] The Norfolk & Western R. R. Co. See Report R. R. Commr. of Va. for 1887, p. 83, etc.

Average rate per ton per mile on all classes of freight (about) . .621 cts.
Average total operating expenses per ton-mile, allotted to freight traffic (about) . . . . . . .382 cts.
Average cost per ton-mile of "conducting transportation" of freight (about) . . . . .148 cts.

The popular opinion very generally entertained is that railroad companies, in charging more for the short-distance non-competitive traffic than for the long-distance competitive traffic, make up by excessive charges upon the former a total or partial loss which they sustain upon the latter. Or at least the fact that they can carry the latter so cheaply at a profit, is thought to demonstrate their ability to carry the former at equally low rates. Mr. Hudson undertakes to prove this by a formula,[1] which, though evidently conclusive to his mind, is really more plausible than sound. He says: "The working expenses of railways in the United States are upon the average 65.21 per cent. of the gross earnings. It is substantially within the margin of 34.79 per cent. of the gross earnings, then, representing the entire net earnings of the road, that a variation of rates between points approximately equal in distance might be made without incurring actual and direct loss in each single transaction."

The fallacy of the argument consists in the assumption that the cost of each single transaction, as the business is more and more enlarged, is as great as the cost of the same transaction where the business is very limited. This is contrary to all business experience, and will not stand the test of practical application, as will presently be shown.

If, indeed, the competitive traffic is carried at a loss, the popular opinion above referred to is undoubtedly correct. And where it is carried at any less rate than the

---

[1] "The Railways and the Republic," p. 163.

exigencies of competition force upon the railroad, there is just cause for complaint on the part of the local shipper. He also has just cause of complaint where the company might reduce its local to the level of (or below) its competitive rates, and still earn a reasonable income on the just value of its property. But where the traffic, which would else *go by some other route*, is taken on the *best terms that can be had* by the railroad, *and adds something to the net earnings*, which would otherwise fail to pay a *reasonable income on the just value* of the property,—under these circumstances the opinion is erroneous, and the complaint is not well founded.

That these circumstances frequently exist may be shown by a single practical example. There is a certain road whose average rate per ton per mile is about 1.6 cents, which pays a net income of six per cent on a value of about $20,000 per mile, which is certainly less than the just value of the property. At a certain point on this road it receives a considerable amount of competitive freight, which it is compelled to take at about .8 cent per ton-mile (one half its average rate), or else lose the business. The distance from the point where this freight is received to the terminus of the road where it is delivered is about one hundred miles. In the case under consideration, the road in question receives the competitive freight from a connecting road, in cars belonging to the latter. For the use of those cars it has to pay the company which owns them three fourths of a cent per car for every mile run. The other expenses of taking the competitive freight —in addition to expenses which remain the same whether it is taken or refused—are a few extra clerks and laborers at the points where the freight is taken and delivered, a few additional engines and caboose cars, with the wear and tear upon them, the coal and grease consumed and used, and the pay of the additional train-men. The expense of additional clerks and laborers is so small as to be almost inappreciable when apportioned among all the additional train-loads of freight; and the interest on the cost of additional equipment, when apportioned in the same way, is but trivial.

The "additional expense" of any single train-load of twenty cars, carrying ten tons each, is, practically, 1st, the "car-mileage" paid the connecting road for the use of its cars (which is probably a fair estimate of what the expense would be if the company used its own cars); 2d, wages paid the crew; 3d, coal consumed by the engine; 4th, grease and ordinary wear and tear of engine and caboose.

The receipts for a train-load of cattle (a fair sample of the average rate) carried the 100 miles, at .8 cents per ton per mile, are about	$160.00
Off car mileage, 100 miles and return, at ¾ cents per mile each way on twenty cars; and one caboose, estimated at same cost	$31.50
Wages of crew of five men, aggregate 10 cents per mile each way	$20.00
Coal, ten tons for the round trip, at $2.50 per ton .	$25.00
Grease and ordinary wear and tear (estimated)	$5.00 $81.50
Net earnings on train-load of cattle	$78.50

In the example taken of the cattle train, the train has been supposed to return entirely empty, at a dead loss. If a full or even partial return load can be had—as is frequently the case,—the transaction becomes a much more profitable one. In the foregoing illustration there was no expense to the company of loading, unloading, and handling the competitive traffic. This additional expense, where necessary, of course, diminishes the profit on the transaction; but it is quite evident that a net profit would still remain, even were such expense incurred and deducted from receipts. And yet there is not a single point on the one hundred miles of road over which the competitive freight passes that is charged less than double the rate per ton-mile to the terminus of the road, though the distance traversed is less. But if all rates were reduced to the level of the rate on the competitive traffic, the road would hardly pay expenses; and the same result would follow were the competitive freight refused, unless the local rates are raised to meet the deficiency. In many other occupations besides that of railroad transportation, work is done at a profit far below what would be remunerative if applied to the entire business operations, and yet that work, under the circumstances, undoubtedly increases the net earnings of the business. This is constantly the case in agricultural operations. For example, a farmer, with the arable land at his disposal, and with a very slight increase in the number of laborers, and of farm implements which he must in any event employ and provide, can, in connection with his other crops, profitably produce some commodity, the cultivation of which, if undertaken alone, would actually bring him in debt. So if he has land fit only for pasturage, and pasturage in the neighborhood is abundant and cheap, he can, rather than receive no income from that land, take animals to pasture at any price that will more than pay the actual cost of keeping them. He thus gets a certain additional profit on his fixed capital, and small though that be, it increases the net earnings (or decreases the loss) of his entire farming operations. The illustrations might be multiplied indefinitely.

The roadbed, track etc., of a railroad company are analogous to the land of the farmer. They constitute the fixed capital, and a small additional outlay upon it in wages and equipment will frequently very largely increase the profits of business. Whenever the net revenues of a road are increased by taking competitive traffic, it begins to approach—and very probably reaches—the point where it may reduce local charges, and still have a reasonable income left on the just value of its property.

One of the most important functions of public railway regulation is to see that when that point is reached, a reduction in local charges is begun. And as the net revenues are more and more increased, the local rates should be brought more and more into harmony with the through or competitive rates. Paradoxical as it may seem on the first blush, reflection leads to the conclusion that the practice of charging less for the longer than the shorter haul, *under the limitations which have been suggested*, confers upon the less-favored communities a portion of the benefits which the most-favored enjoy in the matter of transportation. It tends to a diffusion and equilibrium of commercial advantages between communities which have no apparent connection with one another.

If, for example, the Chesapeake & Ohio, by fixing its competitive rates from western points at a very low figure, can get a portion of the traffic which would otherwise pass over the trunk lines north of the Ohio and Potomac rivers,—and increases its net earnings by doing so,—it can to that extent reduce its local charges. And so the profits of that traffic which would else go to other companies, and enure to the benefit of the communities which they serve, in effecting a general reduction of transportation charges along their lines, is diverted to the C. & O., and should enure to the benefit of the local communities served by the latter, by making possible a reduction of local charges.

A singular, and in some respects beneficial, result of low long-haul rates is the introduction of competition between the manufactures or other products of different regions or communities where otherwise monopoly might prevail. This not only effects a reduction of prices to the consumers, but frequently enables a selection to be made between different varieties of the same general class of articles, according as the style of manufacture and class of work may differ in one place from another. For example, wagons made in Nashville, Tennessee, may be sold in Racine, Wisconsin, and the Racine-made wagon may be sold in Tennessee.[1] The products of southern and eastern factories may be laid down in competition with those of northern and western factories, at the very doors of the latter, and *vice versa*.

To accomplish this result, the transportation of any commodity over a long distance, and into the territory of a competitive commodity, must usually be at a very low rate, and is probably often less than the charge for a shorter distance over the same line and in the same direction. The justification of the practice, where such is the case, must depend upon the principles just discussed. It is an example of competitive traffic. And it is, as before remarked, one of the most important functions of public railway regulation, to see to it that local communities, where competition does not prevail, receive the benefit of lower rates, to which they are entitled as the net earnings from competitive traffic are more and more increased.

From the foregoing analysis it may perhaps be inferred that the railroad companies, by applying the principles there laid down, will always, when called to account, be able to justify the unpopular and apparently unreasonable practice of charging more for the shorter than for the longer transportation over the same line. No doubt,

---

[1] See vol. i., Interstate Com. Reports, p. 224 (testimony).

in very many cases the practice may be justified,—at least to a great extent. But it is equally certain that the practice is frequently carried to an unwarranted and unjustifiable extreme; as, for example, where the inequality between the long- and short-haul rate is such that freights can be carried from the original point of shipment, *away from their destination*, to a competitive point, and then shipped *back again, through the starting-point*, to ultimate destination.[1]

It is also undoubtedly a fact that competition is often carried to an extent which the exigencies of the case do not really warrant, as in the case of wars of rates, so common among competing lines.

In the heat of these conflicts transportation charges between competitive points are reduced to figures which are astonishingly and sometimes ruinously low. But in the absence of specific legislation to the contrary, the business of intermediate places is granted no reduction, and consequently suffers the most serious disadvantage. Where all the rivals are equally responsible for the existence of hostilities, it may be well enough to punish, and, as far as possible, to curb them all, by the application of the long- and short-haul rule. But the existence and strict enforcement of a law forbidding a greater charge for the shorter than the longer transportation has not apparently operated in any great degree to prevent rate wars between competing lines.

---

[1] See 1st Interstate Com. Reports, p. 108 (testimony).

And it may happen that a single line will recklessly (or perhaps maliciously) institute a cut of rates which its more conservative rivals are compelled, however reluctantly, to follow, or else to lose considerable business to which their situation justly entitles them.

Under these circumstances, to punish all for the misconduct or folly of one, seems hard. On the other hand, the protection of the public against unnecessary discrimination should certainly be paramount to the protection of rival carriers against each other. To protect the public without doing injustice to the companies, the long-and-short-haul law should be coupled with authority in a commission to see that no carrier shall make unreasonably low rates at competitive points. Not only in such flagrant cases as have just been suggested, is public intervention proper and necessary to prevent the perpetration of injustice and wrong, but in less glaring instances it may perhaps be advantageously applied. For it seems to be the case that railroad managers—owing to their engrossment in the effort to secure competitive business—frequently neglect the interests of the local communities, which they regard as peculiarly their own property. Experience has shown that reduction of local charges often so increases the volume of local traffic as to result in an ultimate increase of net earnings from that source. And there are instances where roads, cut off from their through traffic by hostile combinations, have turned their attention to developing and fostering the interests of their local communities, with results of the most beneficial character to all concerned.

For a time this policy may prove unprofitable, or may be attended with actual loss, but it has seldom failed to bring its reward, not only in the shape of increased net revenues, but by establishing with patrons of the road relations of cordiality and a sense of mutual interest and benefit, in place of the enmity and sense of injury which an apparent disregard of the local interests has so frequently engendered.

Another kind of discrimination between localities which may be briefly noticed here, is what is known as the " rebilling privilege."[1] This consists in allowing to the jobbers of a city or town which the railway chooses to make a distributing point, the right to forward to their customers in other places consignments which the jobbers have first received, at the same rates as would have been charged had the shipment been in the first instance direct from the place of consignment to ultimate destination. That is, the sum of the charges for the two shipments— 1st, from the original consignor to the jobber in the favored town, and, 2d, from that town to the consignee of the jobber—is only what the charge would have been had there been a single shipment from the first consignor to the last consignee.

A city enjoying this privilege evidently has a great advantage in the distribution of freights over a rival city or

---

[1] See testimony, Cullom Committee, p. 1435.

town from which the regular local rates are charged to points in adjacent territory, upon similar consignments, forwarded under similar circumstances. The charges for the two shipments would generally, of course, aggregate considerably more than the charge for the single through shipment.

The "milling in transit" system which prevails largely in the northwest, and to some extent elsewhere, involves the same principle, and confers a similar advantage. This consists in allowing to milling establishments located on the line of a road between the grain-producing regions and the flour-markets, the privilege of bringing their wheat to the mills, converting it into flour, and forwarding the flour to market, at the same rate—or nearly the same—as is charged for carrying the wheat direct from place of production to place of consumption. While the same right is granted to all milling towns, and all establishments along the line, this practice is perhaps not objectionable. But where the privilege is allowed to some places or persons, to the exclusion of others, it constitutes an unjustifiable and ruinous discrimination.

CHAPTER VI.

Personal Discriminations—Resulting from Excessive Competition; from Supposed Advantages to Accrue to the Railroads Therefrom ; from Mere Favoritism—Never Justifiable—Distinguished from Local Discriminations—Difficulty of Detection—The Pooling System—Differential Rates—Unnecessary Railroad Building—Division of Territory—Consolidations—Discrimination between Different Kinds of Traffic, or Classification of Freight—Value and Risk, and Not Cost of Service, the Basis of Classification—Necessity to the Public Welfare of the Adoption of this Basis—Abuses.

ANOTHER evil that gradually grew and became incorporated into the operation of railroads, is that of discrimination between individuals in the prices charged for transportation, and in facilities afforded. These personal discriminations, though not wholly confined to competitive points, were largely developed by the struggle between railroads for competitive business. In many cases, however, they appear to be entirely arbitrary. For instance, it was proven before the Hepburn Committee, that the New York Central Railroad gave to one shipper a rate of ten cents a hundred from New York to Syracuse, while other shippers were charged rates varying from sixteen to thirty cents a hundred for the same service. Discriminations of this sort are usually effected by means of rebates or drawbacks on the regular (or open) rates, and at competing points are (or were) almost universally practised by railroad companies in favor of large shippers.

The great corporations, in order to secure the business, vie with one another in giving these rebates (which, as a rule, is secretly done), until finally the evil culminates in an open and furious war of rates over competitive business. "Before the Southwestern Railroad Association was formed, the several roads extending from Chicago and St. Louis, and other Mississippi River points to Kansas City, Leavenworth, Atchison, and St. Joseph, indulged in frequent struggles for the competitive traffic, the inevitable result of which was that the published tariff was disregarded, and special or contract rates became the rule. Thus, while the tariff from Chicago to Kansas City, on the first four classes (of freight) was 90, 70, 50, and 30 cents per hundred pounds respectively, large shippers had contracts at one half the rates above-named, while a few secured contracts at even less than the rates last described. For example, a merchant might think he has done well to secure a first-class rate of 45 cents a hundred from Chicago to Kansas City, and 30 cents from St. Louis, until he learned incidentally that his rival in the same trade had obtained rates 10 cents per hundred weight lower. . . . Under such circumstances, none but the unwary paid tariff rates. The alert shippers—and the large ones come under that head—were shrewd enough to work one road against another, exciting their jealousies and suspicions, until those having freight to forward were able to name the price at which it should be carried."[1] In the graphic language of Mr. Haines, a prominent southern railroad manager: "This system went on from bad to worse, centering the business of competitive points in fewer hands, drawing the business of neighboring stations to competitive points, and rendering it impracticable for a man with small capital to establish himself in business under such disadvantages. . . . The railroad managers no longer controlled their own business. Under the threat of losing business they were forced to make concessions which they knew were wrong. They were annoyed by applications which it was impolitic to refuse, and met with suspicion and treachery from the very men who were being made rich by rebates, and yet feared that some one else might be getting better rates."[2] The situation resulting from competition between railroads has been described by Mr. Adams, whose experience formerly as head of the Massachusetts Railroad Commission, and now as head of the Union Pacific Railroad Company, entitles his utterances to great respect, as follows: "Besides all this, however, competition led to favoritism of the grossest character. Men or business firms whose shipments by rail were large could command their own terms, as compared to those whose business was small. The most

---

[1] J. W. Midgley in Appendix to Rept. of Cullom Com., p. 226.
[2] *Id.*, p. 132.

irritating as well as wrongful inequalities were thus made common all over the land. Every local settlement and every secluded farmer, saw other settlements and other farmers more fortunately placed, whose consequent prosperity seemed to make their own ruin a question of time. Place to place, or man to man, they might compete; but where the weight of the railroad was flung into one scale it was strange, indeed, if the other did not kick the beam."[1] These wars of rates over competitive business logically result in aggravation of discriminations against local shippers. During a period when rates on the former went down to a point where they failed to pay perhaps even the bare cost of movement, the New York Central Company continued to pay regular dividends on stock. That, it is said, they were enabled to do from the fact that while they were carrying competitive traffic at an absolute loss, they had such complete control of their local traffic that they recouped the losses upon the former by charges upon the latter, which were excessively exorbitant during the same period.[2] Nor are these personal discriminations always confined to competitive points. For example, during one of the trunk-line railway wars every miller, *with one exception*, at Black Rock and Niagara, on the New York Central, had to close his mill, being unable to get his flour to New York as cheaply as the millers of Minneapolis, in the far west. The answer given to the

---

[1] " Railroads : Their Origin and Problems," p. 125.
[2] Testimony, Cullom Committee, p. 66.

millers who inquired how it was that one of them alone could maintain his commercial existence, was that that particular miller had put in the newest machinery and had the best-stocked mill, and therefore could afford to undersell his neighbors in the markets of New York. The confession was, however, extracted from that miller before the Hepburn Committee, that he had a special contract with the railroad company, which was to continue only on condition of its being kept secret, by which he had the rate on his flour prorated with the rate from Minneapolis. It has sometimes been claimed that the large shipper should have lower rates than the smaller shipper, on the same principle that the wholesale purchaser of goods obtains lower prices than the retail purchaser. But the best railroad authorities concede that where one or more entire car-loads are shipped, the price should be proportioned to the quantity. And it has been strongly argued in favor of commercial cities, anxious to extend their retail trade, that provided the car be loaded to its capacity, and all its contents destined to the same point, car-load rates should be given, though the contents are consigned to different persons.[1] The latter proposition is partially admitted, and the former is established by the testimony of Albert Fink, the head of the Trunk Line Association, before the Hepburn Committee, in the following language:

" In the case of shipments on railroads in less than car-

---

[1] Testimony, Senate Committee, p. 872, etc.

loads, the cost will be greater than full car-load shipments —not always, but as a rule. Cars cannot be fully loaded when a number of small shipments are made, which have to be unloaded at different stations. After unloading one shipment at an intermediate station, the train has to proceed with the smaller load, but without reducing expenses in proportion. It is therefore proper that the shipper should pay the additional cost. There is good ground for discriminating between small and large shipments. But where shipments are made by the car-load, where it is merely a question of one or more car-loads, no additional cost is incurred by the railroad company. Whether these shipments are made by one or by many shippers, it costs the same. It costs no more to ship ten car-loads of freight between two stations, whether they belong to one shipper or to ten shippers; whether one man ships ten car-loads, or ten men ship one car-load each. There is no ground for discriminating in favor of the large shipper. Any discrimination made in his favor is entirely arbitrary. There is no rule, no principle, on which it can be established or defended. All arbitrary discrimination works injustice to others. Take a flour-mill producing ten car-loads of flour a day, and alongside of it at the same station, a mill producing only a car-load. The railroad company decides that it gives to the larger mill a rebate of twenty-five cents a barrel. This of itself constitutes a fair profit. The large mill can undersell the small mill in any market in which they are competitors. It can sell at cost and make twenty-five cents a barrel, while the other mill, if it wants to sell, must sell without any profit at all. This leads to the breaking up of the small establishment, and the railroad is the instrument through which it is accomplished."

That the railroad (a public highway) should thus be made the instrument to build up one individual and break down another, is a thing never contemplated and not to be tolerated. Of course there must be instances where the cost of service is so much greater in proportion, in case of the small shipment than in that of the large, that a larger proportionate charge for the small shipment would be perfectly justifiable; as where a single animal is shipped in a car to itself. Here the cost to the railroad is but little less than the cost of a fully loaded car would be. In fact, as will be shown in subsequent pages, a lesser charge proportionately on car-loads is generally proper. But where several small shipments of the same character of freight, all destined to the same point, though perhaps consigned from and to as many different persons, can by judicious management be united in a single car-load, the additional cost would not be sufficient to warrant an additional charge. Some sacrifice should, if necessary, be made by the carrier, to secure equality between shippers. Where, as is sometimes the case, a rebate or other concession is made to a large shipper out of all proportion to the lesser cost of service, the practice is still more unjustifiable. Where the concession is made on purely personal grounds, no pretext of excuse can be given for it. But it is sometimes sought to be justified on the ground that a greater aggregate volume of traffic can be obtained by concessions to large shippers, and the revenues of the company thus increased.

Whether this be the fact or not, it does not justify the practice. It still results in crushing out the smaller shipper. It bears no analogy to the practice of charging more for the short than for the long haul, which, as has been shown, is, under some circumstances and conditions, justifiable.

In the latter case, it is true, the local point suffers from the unequal position in which it is placed, but the inequality results, not from the voluntary action of the railroad company, but from the existence of other routes of transportation.

It exists independently of the railroad, and the latter simply takes things as it finds them and makes the best of them. The inequality of the local point is not thereby increased, and may be diminished. But the inequality in favor of the larger shipper arises from the voluntary act of the railroad company, and can only result in detriment to the small shipper. There is no extraneous compulsion which forces the railroad into the practice, as there is in the case of the long and short haul, and to create this inequality for the purpose merely of increasing revenues, is to rob the railroad of the character of a public highway.

The most flagrant and notorious instance of discrimination between shippers is that long practised by the leading railroads of the country in favor of the Standard Oil Company. It commenced at a time when the struggle for competitive business between the trunk lines was unusually violent and almost incessant. Each railroad company vied with the others in offering the utmost concessions to secure the enormous and valuable freight of the Standard Company.

Finally an agreement was entered into between the Standard and the principal competing roads, whereby in consideration of a large concession made by the carrying companies in the rates for transporting the shipments of the Standard Company, the latter undertook to apportion its freight among the several competitors, that each might have a share. This seemed better for the transportation companies than the existence of constant and costly warfare over traffic which perhaps was frequently carried at less than cost. At the same time it gave the Standard such an advantage over all competitors as enabled it to monopolize the vast proportion of the oil-refining business of the country. In the space of less than two years the Standard is said to have received, in the shape of rebates from the railway companies, no less than ten million dollars.[1] Finally its resources became so great, and its control over the petroleum product so complete, that it assumed, successfully, to dictate its own terms for the transporta-

---

[1] See "The Railways and the Republic," ch. iii., entitled "The History of a Commercial Crime."

tion of its oil. In one instance it went so far, under threat of withdrawing its business from a railroad company, as to demand that the latter should carry its oil at ten cents per barrel, should charge all other shippers thirty-five cents per barrel, and should pay the Standard twenty-five cents per barrel of the amount received from other shippers! (See Report of Cullom Committee, p. 199.)

Discrimination of this kind—that is, between individuals similarly situated—is necessarily unjust, and should be strictly prohibited by law, regardless of whether the revenues of the road will be injuriously affected or not.

Equality of rights to every member of the community should be paramount to the profits of the carrier. But this species of discrimination assumes various disguises where there is legislation forbidding it, and the railroad companies choose to obey the letter of the law and yet violate its spirit. As said by Mr. Fink, the discrimination can be made in a thousand different forms. "It may be made through reductions in the weight, charging for less than the actual weight, or by a donation to a shipper. If he ships by a line for a year, and he has been a very good customer, the company can make him a Christmas gift. And so the law may be evaded in a thousand ways. It is almost impossible to discover these evasions, and you cannot punish them before you discover them."[1]

The practice of misrepresenting the weight or the char-

---

[1] Testimony, Cullom Committee, p. 122.

acter of goods to be forwarded over railroads has recently attracted considerable attention.

"This practice has been in operation for a long time, but since the enactment of the Interstate Commerce law it has greatly increased, and has, in a great measure, taken the place of the payment of rebates. . . . There are two distinct features of this practice to be noted: 1. When the motive of the shipper is simply to cheat the railroad companies. . . . 2. When freight is under-billed, or the character of goods misrepresented, by an understanding, direct or implied with the carriers, to secure the business of certain shippers in competition with other carriers;—thus favoring one shipper as against another. . . . It may be said that so far as the railroads themselves are concerned, they are able to protect themselves against this misrepresentation by examining and weighing all goods. This is true to a certain extent. . . . But if it were practicable to weigh and examine freights at all points, and secure a proper check, another difficulty would be encountered, namely: there are always some roads which will not join their competitors in adopting a system of weighing and inspection. While such roads are willing that other roads should exercise a strict supervision over shipments, they, in order to secure the goodwill of the shippers and increased traffic, refuse to adopt the same measures. Consequently, the other competing roads have to do likewise, or go out of the business."[1]

---

[1] See letter of Albert Fink to Senator Cullom of March 15, 1888.—"Interstate Commerce Debate, in 50th Congress," p. 24.

The practice of underbilling has been thoroughly examined by the Interstate Commerce Commission, and its unfairness and injurious results fully explained.[1] A common method of evading a law against rebates is thus described by Mr. Charles Francis Adams, Jr.: "It is what is known as the free-pass system. . . . There has been no book rebate given in that case, and no drawback paid. Nothing can be found out. . . . The extent to which this abuse has grown is very alarming."[2] Discriminations have also frequently been accomplished under the guise of paying commissions to agents for procuring freights by solicitation,—the agents dividing commissions with the shippers. The device for securing business by paying commissions to agents is practised more generally in passenger traffic, and has at times been carried to the verge of a public scandal. But there is reason to believe that it has been largely availed of by some roads in the freight department, and though the agent may be required to certify that he has not divided commissions with the shippers, a strong suspicion, to say the least, may well be entertained that this is frequently done. Where, as is not infrequently the case, heavy shippers of some peculiar product or commodity, requiring special kinds of cars for the safest and most convenient transportation, own the cars in which their freight is carried, and the railway companies pay to the owners a mileage or per diem for their use, it is easy

---

[1] 2d Report of Interstate Commerce Commission, p. 813.
[2] Testimony, Cullom Committee, pp. 1218 and 1362.

to see that an unjust discrimination, in favor of or between such car owners, may be effected by varying the amount of mileage or per diem paid to different shippers. The charge for transportation may be the same to each of two shippers of dressed meat or petroleum, but if one of them is allowed one cent per mile for his car, and the other but three fourths of one cent, the discrimination is as plain and as unjust as if it were upon the freight itself.

Railroad companies may sometimes get an ample return for special favors to shippers, in the aid afforded by the latter to prevent legislation directed against unpopular railroad practices, or intended to subject them more completely to public regulation.

Legislation of this kind, it is asserted, was defeated in New York by a combination between the railroad companies and their favored shippers.[1] Instances of this sort occurring in their own experience will suggest themselves to those who have had part in such legislative attempts.

The railroads themselves, as well as shippers, have suffered—even to bankruptcy, often—by the fierceness of the competition, and the consequent reduction of rates to and from competing points, frequently to merely nominal figures. They have sought to remedy the evil by devising the "*pooling system.*" This may be briefly described as the result of a combination among the railroads to maintain rates at competitive points, for the pool never embraces local traffic. The original agreements among the com-

---

[1] Testimony, Cullom Committee, p. 292.

panies were simply for the maintenance of rates, and provided no means of enforcing the obedience of the parties to the agreement. And such agreements have long been and are still in successful operation, where the number of competing lines and of competitive points are comparatively few. An example is the "Associated Railways of Virginia and the Carolinas," whose object is the maintenance of agreed rates at competitive points, without any pool, allowing the traffic to find its own channels.[1] But, as the law discountenances combinations of this character, as being in restraint of competition and against its own policy, the courts would not enforce compliance with these agreements, and consequently, in most cases, they were violated wherever the immediate interests of any of the parties seemed to make the violation advantageous. The multiplicity of subordinate agents of the different competing roads and their connections forming "through fast freight lines," each striving to secure his "share of the business" for his particular line, rendered the maintenance of rates, under a simple agreement between the principal officers of the road, practically impossible.[2] It was obvious that these agreements must be maintained, however, to prevent ruinous rate wars, and hence arose the necessity of devising some means of binding the parties to them, in the absence of any legal obligation.

The money pool and the traffic pool were then resorted

---

[1] Vol. i. Interstate Commerce Repts., p. 125.
[2] Testimony, Cullom Committee, p. 1210. App. to Rept. Cullom Committee, p. 237., etc.

to. Under the former the total earnings of all the lines from competitive traffic are divided in certain fixed proportions among all the members of the pooling association. A joint fund contributed by the pooled lines, sufficient for the purpose, is periodically placed under the control of the pool commissioner, who applies it to produce the ratios of earnings among the several lines contemplated by the agreement. In this way an excess of earnings above its agreed ratio made by one line, is transferred by the commissioner out of the funds under his control to the line or lines which have earned less than their ratio. There is thus an agency outside of the railroads themselves, created by them, but independent of any number less than a majority of them, which makes equal the inequalities arising in the independent operation of the several associated roads. And by this means the natural inclination of any one road to increase its business and earnings by cutting under the others is to a large extent restrained. In the traffic pool the whole competitive traffic itself is divided among the members of the pool according to certain fixed ratios. For this purpose the pool commissioner is authorized to have freight, which is brought to the depot of one line for transportation over it, transferred, when necessary to produce the agreed ratios of traffic, to the depots of another line for transit over the latter. The traffic pool seems to be preferred by railroad managers, as more effective than the money pool, but the diversion of freights which it necessitates has given rise to considerable complaint from shippers.[1] Circumstances, however, frequently exist which permit the diversion of traffic to be effected without encountering this trouble.

The ratio of earnings or of tonnage to which each road is entitled in the pool is determined by what it would naturally obtain, in the absence of any agreement and of any special inducements offered to obtain the competitive traffic. If the parties interested cannot agree upon this, the question is referred to arbitration. The agreement or award is generally made binding for the period of at least one year, the object being to impart to the contract the element of permanency.[2] It is amazing how nearly the natural share of each road in the traffic is thus approximated. This is evidenced by the fact that of the immense west-bound tonnage from New York City, consigned via the different lines of the associated roads in 1884, only 2.6 per cent. was diverted to produce the agreed ratios.

Intimately connected with the subject of pooling is that of differential rates, established and agreed upon between competing carriers. The right to make lower charges, or "differentials," on competitive traffic is conceded by the more advantageously situated and better equipped of the associated roads to those whose routes are less desirable, attractive, or efficient. In

---
[1] Testimony, Cullom Committee, pp. 14, 119, 132, *et seq.*
[2] Report of Cullom Committee, Appendix, p. 227.

this way the weaker lines are permitted, in a certain sense, to "buy business," and the differentials are so calculated as to enable each of the different lines to procure as nearly as possible its agreed percentage of traffic, by direct consignments from shippers, and without actual diversion of freights from the routes over which they may have been consigned. This allowance of differentials is a very common practice among associated traffic routes in the handling of competitive business. It presents one of the apparent anomalies of railroad practice, which is that the poorest and weakest roads—those least able to furnish cheap transportation—do in fact carry the competitive traffic at the lowest charges, and to a certain extent determine the charges which their stronger rivals shall impose. The weak lines, in order to get a considerable volume of the business, may, for reasons heretofore explained, afford to make very considerable concessions on competitive traffic; and the greater the concessions the greater will be the amount of traffic diverted from the stronger lines. So that to the latter the alternatives are presented of either losing a large amount of business, or entering on a costly rate war, or conceding a differential to the weaker route, by which it may secure a satisfactory share of the traffic. Differentials may exist without pools, the pool being merely a method of maintaining them in force as agreed upon.

Another provision usually contained in pooling compacts is that against interchanging traffic with any connecting road which refuses to abide by the rules and regulations of the association in the matter of rates, classifications, etc.¹

The means adopted for the rapid, convenient, and inexpensive interchange of traffic are the "fast freight lines" or "dispatch lines," which are simply associations of several independent railroads for the transportation of freight, which in its transit from starting-point to destination must pass over two or more of the associated roads. Each road furnishes a certain number of cars, designated as "line cars," which are carried through over all the associated roads, or such portion of them as may be necessary, without breaking bulk or transferring contents. Generally each of the associated roads furnishes its own train-men and motive power for so much of the transit as is over its own line. Each road pays a fixed sum per mile for each car belonging to other members of the association which passes over its track. The car mileage is reported to a central office, where balances arising from the unequal use by one road of cars belonging to others are adjusted and settled. A common through rate is agreed upon by all the members of the association, and each one usually receives a share thereof proportioned to the distance traversed over its own line, compared with the whole distance over which the freight is carried. Thus the "dispatch line," though composed of a number of different and independent roads, is, for

---

¹ See Report of Cullom Committee, Appendix, p. 237, *et seq.*

all the purposes contemplated in its organization, practically one single railroad. Prior to the establishment of these lines, the freight was transferred at the terminus of each road.[1] It is easy to see the complete control a road terminating at a great port may have over interior roads dependent upon it for an outlet, by refusing to admit them to membership of a "dispatch line" on a pro rata basis, and demanding, if not a transfer of freight to its own cars, at least an "arbitrary" compensation for the transportation over its own line.

With this brief explanation of the object and methods of railway pools, and of the devices for enforcing them, it is to be said that both these methods of pooling (*i. e.*, the money and the traffic pool) have been found effective for the accomplishment of their main purpose —the maintenance of rates and the prevention of unjust discriminations—in inverse proportion to the number of roads embraced in the pool, or "affiliating" with the several pooled lines. As the number has increased it has become more difficult to satisfy different interests, and to apply the artificial and self-imposed restraints provided to maintain the organization.[2] The advocates of the pooling system have accordingly of late been arguing in favor of legalizing the system, in the interest, as it is asserted, of the general public as well

---

[1] See Report on Internal Commerce, U. S. 1886, pp. 680, 681, where an interesting history of the origin of the "dispatch lines" is given by Mr. C. A. Sindall, Secretary of the Southern Railway & Steamship Association.

[2] Testimony, Cullom Committee, p. 104.

as of the railroads. Compliance with the agreements might then be judicially enforced, and they would of course be much more effective. The primary object of pooling, it may be conceded, has been to protect and promote the interests of the railroad companies by checking competition, and the public welfare was probably by no means the leading consideration with the originators of the system. But it has been shown how the manifest tendency of competition, at points where that principle has free play, is to raise rates at local or non-competitive points. In the absence of public regulation of transportation, this may almost be said to be the necessary result. The instability in rates, and the personal discriminations—often so difficult of detection—arising from unchecked competition, have also been adverted to.

Pooling, therefore, so long as the agreements can be fairly maintained, manifestly tends to remove one of the principal causes, of local as well as personal discriminations. This is admitted even by Mr. Sterne, one of the best informed and ablest critics of railroad practices.[1] And it is hardly fair to say (what the common law assumes) that the pooling system is necessarily antagonistic to the public interest. The principle of the law which is supposed to put agreements of this character beyond its pale, is based upon the fear that extortionate charges will be imposed upon the public.

But the fact seems to be that the strength of a pool is

---

[1] Testimony, Cullom Committee, p. 72.

in a certain sense a source of danger to its permanence. If such charges are imposed by it as to swell the profits inordinately, combinations are formed to share in them. Circuitous routes may be opened to be closed for a consideration ; new competing lines will be built which must be taken into the pool, reducing the earnings of each line, but not resulting in a permanent reduction of rates.[1] These considerations, as well as the limitation usually imposed by the existence of water competition, would seem to be a powerful conservator of reasonable rates on the pooled business. The pool no doubt facilitates the imposition of relatively high charges on certain classes of traffic, as will be hereafter explained, but the overwhelming weight of testimony justifies the assertion that, as a rule, the rates on pooled traffic have been reasonable and equitably adjusted, and been brought into comparatively harmonious relations with local rates.

There is, however, an instance which, not very long ago, attracted public attention, where the Union Pacific Railroad at the dictation of the Colorado pool, of which it was a member, deliberately imposed prohibitory rates on the transportation of steel rails intended for the construction of a railroad which would be a rival and competitor of one of the associated roads. In the same connection may be mentioned the refusal of the roads in the Colorado pool, to interchange traffic with an independent road which sought an outlet for its business over some of the

---

[1] Report of Cullom Committee, Appendix, p. 230.

pooled roads. The refusal arose from the fact that the independent road in question was a direct competitor of one member of the pool. Certain litigation arising from it has heretofore been adverted to, and the power of the legislature to compel the mutual interchange of traffic under such circumstances has been discussed.

This arbitrary conduct of the Colorado pool illustrates the necessity of public regulation of these associations. But, on the whole, the public benefit derived from the pooling system seems greatly to outweigh the danger of public detriment from its existence. Perhaps so long as railroad companies continue to enjoy an absolute monopoly of transportation over their own lines, so that free competition is restricted in its operation to a comparatively few favored points, it may be worthy of serious consideration, whether it would not be better to legalize than to prohibit pooling—taking care to put the whole matter under strict public supervision and control. The companies would then be left comparatively free to bring their local rates into something like harmony with the long-distance rates, and should they fail to do so where the needs of the local community and their own revenues make it proper to be done, then it is the function of public regulation to compel it to be done. In this way legalized railway pooling might be made the most effective aid to public railway regulation.

The public encouragement usually given to the building of railroads in this country, and the apparent prosperity of an existing pool, even where no serious and well grounded complaint exists against it, has sometimes enabled railroad projectors to procure large sums from investors for the construction of an additional competing line. The consequence perhaps may be heavy financial losses to investors in the new road which undertakes an unequal contest with existing lines, as well as a considerable impairment of the revenues of the latter. A matter of more public importance is the disturbance of the business equilibrium, which the injection of this new element into the situation occasions. The most conspicuous example of this kind of speculative railroad construction is the West Shore road from New York to Buffalo. It is generally conceded that there was little or no occasion of public utility for this road, for it was so located with reference to the New York Central, as to serve almost exactly the same communities, both local and competitive, that the latter already served in an efficient and acceptable manner. It at once entered upon a career of reckless competition and underbidding for traffic, which the Central was compelled to meet. The action of the latter deranged to a greater or less extent the entire trunk-line association. No public good of substantial duration was accomplished; on the contrary, a railroad war with its concomitant evils of instability in rates and unjust discrimination was precipitated upon the country. The West Shore soon became financially wrecked, passed into the hands of receivers, and, after being operated for a number of years at an enormous deficiency below expenses, was finally absorbed by the Central and taken into the pool. The result of the whole transaction, so far as the general public was concerned, was that the cost of the West Shore was added to the aggregate capitalization upon which the pooled lines sought to make a profit. No new traffic of consequence was reached, and the manifest tendency must have been to increase rates, wherever such a course would result in increased net earnings.

The best thought on both sides of the railroad question (as illustrated, for example, by Mr. Sterne and Mr. Fink) seems to recognize the advisability of legislative inquiry into the public necessity for any proposed new road, before granting a charter for its construction.

In some jurisdictions where a free railroad law exists, and no special act of incorporation is necessary, the unrestrained construction of railroads has been carried to an injurious length, as in the case of the West Shore. But the uselessness of the proposed new road for the accomplishment of any public good should be very clearly made out to warrant the refusal of a charter. As a general thing, the more railroads are multiplied, the greater becomes the number of competing points, and the more uniform and pervasive the principle of competition. At all events, whether a proposed new line shall be built or not, is a question for determination by the public, and not by the officials of existing routes with which it will compete. But it appears, from the action of the Colorado pool above noticed, that the heads of existing lines sometimes take the matter into their own hands. They would probably plead the general law of self-defence in justification of their action, but the plea certainly would not be admissible.

In the trunk-line association differentials are established between routes from the common territory to different seaboard cities, as well as between directly competing roads having both termini in common. The principle of differentials between cities is the reverse of that between roads. Under this arrangement the terminal city whose route to the common territory is shortest and most advantageous receives a lower rate than those more remotely situated. Thus the rate from the West to Baltimore is lowest, and that to Boston highest. This advantage to the shortest route is supposed to be compensated, as far as the export trade is concerned, by the superior export facilities provided at the termini of the longer routes. The question of differential rates between cities is one of great difficulty, and has been the occasion of furious railroad wars. It seems impossible to satisfy the claims of the commercial rivals.

In the case of Boston, where the differential rate is not compensated by superior export facilities, a rebate from the regular rate is allowed on western products exported from that port. This is necessary to enable Boston to hold its export trade, which would otherwise go to New

York—thus cutting off that much traffic from the roads tributary to Boston, and diverting it to the roads tributary to New York. So that with the railroads the question is largely one of revenue to themselves, not merely of favor to the port. The importance attached to this rebate provision by the commercial interests of the city of Boston is shown by the remarks of Senator Hoar in the debates on the Interstate Commerce Bill.[1]

Under the pooling principle of allotting percentages to the different associated lines in accordance with the share of the traffic which each would naturally receive,—distance, location, terminal facilities, reasonable differentials, etc., being considered,—it is plain that there may be competing lines which on that basis would get none of the traffic.

Such a line may prefer to keep out of the pool, in order to obtain by rebates and by cutting under the pool rates the business it could not get by maintaining them. Whether or not a new competitor shall be admitted into a traffic association, depends on whether the business and revenues of the latter are so far disturbed or diminished by the undercutting of the former, as to make it worth while to give it such a portion of the tonnage or earnings as will afford it more net revenue than it can derive from the pursuit of an independent policy.

Unity of action among the stronger lines, it is said, enables them to ignore certain elements of competition

---

[1] See *Cong. Rec.*, 1886–7, p. 692, *et seq.*

which would otherwise occasion serious disturbance.[1] But the constant extension of railway lines must from time to time force upon existing associations the recognition of new competitors. For instance, the Chesapeake & Ohio, which was never a member of any of the pools, has long had western connections in the country tributary to the trunk-lines, and it has access to northern and eastern cities, *via* lines extending north through Virginia, and *via* Newport News, its tidewater terminus. This road has always had some traffic between western points and northern and eastern points, which it must have secured by giving rates considerably lower than those given by any of the trunk lines[2]; and it has probably made some money (*i. e.*, increased its net earnings) by this traffic. But the amount of business diverted from the trunk lines has not heretofore been sufficient to compel the admission of the C. & O. into the association. Recently completed connections have, however, put the C. & O. on a much better footing for competition than it has heretofore occupied, and recently, it is said, it has been formally recognized as a member of the trunk-line association, to the extent of being allowed differentials on certain portions of the competitive business.

A method by which competition between railroads may be prevented, without any agreement to maintain rates, which is the object and essence of pooling, is

---

[1] Testimony, Cullom Committee, p. 751.
[2] See Testimony, Cullom Committee, pp. 751, 752.

by dividing the territory wherein the competition exists. For example, when the Kansas City & Memphis road was built, connecting those cities, it made connections for a tidewater outlet at Norfolk, Va., and began competing for a portion of the seaboard traffic of the trunk lines. To put a stop to this an agreement was entered into, in pursuance of which the Kansas City & Memphis withdrew from its Virginia connection, and made alliances with roads reaching the seaboard further south. And it cut itself off from all traffic originating north of the south line of Virginia and Kentucky by charging high or "local tariff" rates on such business. In consideration of this action the trunk lines cut themselves off from all traffic originating south of the same line by refusing to take it except at "local tariff" rates. The field was thus divided between the competitors by a line running along the southern boundary of Virginia and Kentucky, and the competition was ended. It is difficult to say how far this method might be effectually applied, under more complicated conditions, to supersede the present pooling system. Where the competitors are numerous, as in the case of the trunk lines and their affiliating roads, and the competing points so located with respect to them and to one another, as they are in the country north of the Ohio River for example, the problem would appear to present almost insuperable difficulties. And these difficulties would perhaps be even greater where the traffic of a single city must necessarily be shared in by different lines. It may be, however, that the genius of the men who organized the pool can, if necessary, solve the problem of dividing the field.

The most effectual of all means of destroying competition is by consolidation of the competing lines. And even where consolidation, by actual merger or legal unifying of the companies, is forbidden, the same result may be practically accomplished by the acquisition into the same hands of controlling interests in the stock of the different roads. It has been very forcibly suggested that the prohibition of pooling tends strongly to bring about this state of things. For example, the rail transportation of the territory lying south of the Ohio and Potomac and east of the Mississippi rivers is done principally by six or seven leading companies. The stock of most of these companies is far below par, and Senator Brown of Georgia estimates that $30,000,000 in round numbers would purchase a controlling interest in every one of them. "One single man in the State of New York is able to pay $30,000,000 for the stock, and control the whole of this vast combination. . . . And this would end the necessity for pooling. . . . No pooling is necessary from the Potomac to the Mississippi, and from the coast to the Ohio. As one man controls the railroads in the whole territory, there would be perfect harmony in the management. In other words, the silence of despotism reigns, and the monopoly by combination and consolidation is complete."[1]

---

[1] Senator Brown, *Cong. Rec.*, 1887, p. 608.

By the association of a very limited number of persons, all dominated by a single will and purpose, results precisely similar to that depicted by Senator Brown have again and again been accomplished. And his picture would seem to be highly prophetic of the future. For the manifest tendency of the railroad transportation system is toward centralization, and its results so far as accomplished do not appear generally to have produced public injury. But undoubtedly danger is inherent in such concentration of wealth, and of power over the commerce of the country in a few hands; and these combinations should be brought into such relations with government, or under such governmental regulations, as will preserve for the undiscriminating benefit of all the people, as far as may be, their ever augmenting powers of public good.

The third species of discrimination in charges is that between different kinds of freight or different commodities, and arises from the system of classification of freights. To attempt to fix a separate and distinct price for the transportation of every one of the many hundreds of articles that are daily carried over railroads would manifestly involve very great inconvenience. Accordingly the various commodities of commerce by rail have been divided or classified for greater convenience into a few groups, each one of which embraces many different articles, for the carriage of which nevertheless the same charge is made. This mode of making rates by classification is intended to be for the convenience of the carrier as well as the accommodation of shippers, and long experience has shown that it is the best and most practical way of dealing with the subject. "In making up a class by this method, articles of the same kind are usually grouped together in the same class, as far as this can be done; but as the articles in each class are so very numerous, there is a very great diversity of such articles, and it results that there are generally but few things of the same kind that can be placed in one class."

"As the freight rates of a railroad are laid with a view of obtaining revenue from its operation, it is but just and fair that they should be so distributed among the different articles transported, as far as this can be done, as to bear upon all with relative equality."

It is very evident then that "after all a classification is but a means of arriving at a rate."[1]

In some cases the classification is based upon reasons which at once commend themselves as fair and satisfactory, and though discriminative, cannot be considered unjust. This is the case where the two elements of cost of service and risk alone enter into the classification. Thus more must necessarily be charged for carrying a ton of cotton than a ton of iron ore, more for a car-load of glass-ware than for a car-load of lumber, and more on a package of nitro-glycerine, than on a similar package of

---

[1] See Pyle vs. E.T. V. & G. R. R. Co. 1 Interstate Commerce Reports, p. 771.

soap. In the beginning of railroading very little was known of the "cost of service," *i. e.*, of the different elements entering into the cost of transporting any given article. " It was supposed in a general way that what had been the rates existing on post-roads or highways, pretty well augmented, would be a fair rate on railways. There was no system at all. The first freight tariffs were made because the stage lines or some other line made such and such a rate."[1] The "terminal expenses"—storing in depots, loading, unloading, and handling—enter largely into the question, and great differences arise from the weight and shape of an article of freight. Experience, perhaps, gradually taught the cost of service in transporting different commodities, with an approximation at least to accuracy. But in most instances classification is not based solely or principally on cost of service and risk. Speaking generally, (leaving those elements out of view,) it may be said that the classification of any article of freight is determined by the ratio which the cost of transporting bears to the total cost to the consumer. If the cost of carrying it constitutes a large part of the ultimate price of the article, it is classed low, and the rate is made very little above the bare expense of carriage. On the other hand, if the cost of carriage constitutes but a small part of the ultimate price, the article is classed high, and contributes vastly more to the earnings of the road than its ratable share would be, if the classification were based

---

[1] Gen. Devereux before the Cullom Com. Testimony, p. 826.

on cost of service and risk alone. Actual risk is usually a small element compared with cost of service, and arises from the dangerous and highly destructive, or from the perishable and easily destructible, character of the article, more than from its value. The classification then, practically, is usually based upon the price or value of the article, or in other words, as frequently expressed, upon "what the traffic will bear." The practice of classifying freights upon the basis of value, instead of upon cost of service, is frequently cited by critics of railroad methods as evidence of extortion. And yet it is plain that but for this principle of classification, a vast amount of the commerce of the country, embracing the transportation of many of the necessaries of life from the producer to the consumer, must necessarily cease. Many articles of prime necessity, for manufacture or consumption, such as coal, grain (for long distances), building materials, ores, etc., will not bear transportation, except at figures so low that, while they may enable the railroads to do the business without actual loss, contribute little or nothing to what are called "fixed expenses," such as maintenance of the road, wages, salaries, and interest on investment. Expenses of maintenance, salaries, and wages must of course be paid, or operations will cease, and it is only fair that reasonable profits should be made on the value of the investment. If the effort should be made to assess this low-class traffic with its ratable proportion of all expenses based on cost of service, the result would simply be that transportation of such traffic would cease. The consumer, unable to pay the cost of production and high transportation charges, both of which enter into the cost of the article to him, would seek a substitute either in a different article or from a different field of production. Or if no substitute can be had or no other field of production is more accessible, then the elements entering into the necessary cost of living— that is, food, fuel, and shelter—must be greatly increased in price to the consumer, while decreased in price to the producer.

Inasmuch then as the fixed expenses must be paid, and as a vast class of commodities, which for the good of the whole public must be transported, cannot bear their ratable share of those expenses, it follows that charges of various degrees above their ratable share must be laid on those articles which will bear such charges. This is "charging what the traffic will bear," and rightly understood it is not only not extortion, but entirely justifiable and necessary to the public welfare. The enormously increased volume of traffic which follows upon the policy of low rates on cheap freights, adds largely to the net revenues of the transportation companies; and this, with them, is the direct object had in view. The public benefit resulting from it is merely incidental. It is a case of "a tariff for revenue with incidental protection" to the low-class traffic.

The use to which an article is to be put sometimes determines its classification. For example, fertilizers are frequently classed very low, the object being to cheapen them as much as possible, and encourage their use, in the expectation that the production and consequent shipment of commodities of profitable transportation will be thereby increased.

On the same principle, and with the same object in view, materials to be used in building manufacturing establishments, and raw material intended for conversion into manufactured products, are on some roads classed lower than the same articles intended for other purposes. Sometimes the manufactured product itself may, in the incipiency of a manufacturing enterprise, be classed very low, and be carried for a time almost without profit, until the business is firmly established, and a new source of shipments thus created, when the rates may be raised.

In these cases revenue to the railroad is the prime object, and protection to the favored industry merely the incident. But the same charges must be imposed on all manufactures of the same kind, no matter by whom produced, else the discrimination becomes a mere personal one. In some States indeed, as in Alabama, special contract rates given for the purpose of "developing industrial enterprises," are expressly sanctioned, and excepted from the general anti-discrimination law.

Discrimination in charges between different kinds of traffic based upon principles which have been above noticed and strictly confined to those principles, is not always deserving of censure, and seems frequently to be a necessary condition of railroad transportation, and promotive of the public good. Yet the danger of abuse of these principles is very great ; and there are other cases in which the practice is more questionable, both in its principle and in the consequences which may result from it. Classifications are sometimes established with the avowed purpose of protecting some industry, and not solely or principally to increase the revenues of the companies. Here protection is the principal object in view, and the question of revenue is merely incidental. This is illustrated in the relative classifications of live-stock and dressed meat, which at one time prevailed over the trunk lines from the west to the seaboard. When the executive committee of the trunk-line association met to consider this matter, Mr. Fink distinctly announced that the question before them was how to put the live-stock shippers and the dressed-meat shippers on an equal footing in the eastern markets. In other words, it was how to protect the old-established live-stock business, and the people dependent upon or interested in it, against the advantages which the dressed-meat business with its new processes and appliances would otherwise enjoy. General E. P. Alexander, a high authority on such matters, seems to admit, in his monograph entitled "Railway Practice," (p. 47,) that the controlling consideration with the railway managers, in the decision of that question, was the protection of the live-stock interest, involving, as it does, immense investments and the livelihood of thousands of employés. Very probably the policy pursued by the railway companies in this matter was the best for the public interests. Where two commodities or kinds of traffic are commercially competitive, that is, where they supply the same wants, or are put to the same uses by consumers, the classification should, in the interest of the public and in justice to those directly interested in each commodity, be arranged, as far as circumstances will permit, so that neither commodity shall be enabled, merely by reason of the difference in transportation charges, to supplant the other in the markets, and secure a monopoly. This indeed is in some sense a corollary deducible from the general principle of "charging what the traffic will bear"; but it is to be observed that it may involve considerations entirely outside of the pecuniary interests of the transportation companies themselves. The relative classification of live stock and dressed meat may be wholly or partially justified under the principle just referred to; as they are undoubtedly commodities of a character competitive with each other, each being intended to supply the public demand for the same article of food.

To lower the classification of dressed meat to any considerable extent, would be destructive of the business of shipping beef cattle to market, would entail incalculable injury upon thousands whose living is involved in that business, and would eventually place the meat supply of the large cities in the hands of a few capitalists, who, it may well be imagined, would not be long in organizing a "fresh-meat trust," and eliminating all competition. The protection in this instance has been wisely and beneficially extended, but the subject protected might at any time be changed, with disastrous results to many communities. It seems plain that the question of protection to one industry or another is one for the public and not for the railways to determine. The purely protective policy has very much the appearance of an exercise of powers and functions by the railroad companies wholly beyond the objects of their creation. They were intended as agencies of transportation merely; they have become in large measure the arbiters of many of the most important industries in the country. To leave the control of questions and results of such vast public consequence in their hands, free of all public supervision, would surely be perilous.

The difference between charges on car-loads and less than car-load lots of the same article of freight is usually effected by means of classification—the latter being placed in a higher class than the former. Difference in cost of service is the principle relied on to justify the difference in classification. The greater cost of transporting less than car-load lots is due principally to the fact that, as a rule, the cars cannot be fully loaded, and the weight of paying freight consequently bears a much less ratio to the total weight of a train than is the case where the shipments are by the car-load. Estimates have been made,—which theoretically appear difficult of impeachment,—showing that the cost of carrying less than carload lots of freight is usually at least double the cost of car-loads.[1] The difference in charge is very seldom proportionately as great, and the principle here alluded to seems to afford a sound basis for the lower classification of car-load freight. The argument in its favor, which theoretically appears so strong, is somewhat weakened in practice by the fact that the principle is by no means uniformly adhered to by railroad companies. In the carriage of a great many commodities, no difference per hundred-weight is made between car-loads and less quantities. And there may be cases where the difference in cost is not sufficient to justify the difference in charge, considering the disadvantage at which it places small shippers compared with their competitors in business, who may receive the same character of consignments in car-load lots at the same place, over the same route, and perhaps from the same consignor. It may very likely happen, too, that a greater charge per hundred-weight will be imposed for carrying less than car-loads a shorter distance than is charged for carrying car-loads a longer distance over the same line in the same direction, the shorter being included in the longer distance. This result, so obnoxious to a well-known sentiment, cannot perhaps always be justified by the principle of difference between car-loads and lesser

---

[1] See p. 448 *et seq.* of testimony before Interstate Com. Com., in case of Thurber *et als. vs.* R. R. Cos.

quantities. Nor is the classification by any means always uniform on all lines of road, although, by means of consolidations, despatch lines, and traffic associations, far greater uniformity has been introduced than once prevailed. Sometimes good reasons exist for this lack of uniformity over different lines and in different sections. Thus, where any part of the country produces a great quantity of any particular commodity, as the South does of cotton, for example, and the West of grain, the transportation companies engaged in the movement, on a great scale, of the staple products of the territory which they serve, very properly classify such staples lower than the same commodity may be classified on railroads in other sections, where it constitutes but a small part of the tonnage. But in many cases the difference in the classification of the same article seems incapable of reasonable explanation; and uniformity in the interest of commerce is a great desideratum. It is hardly likely, however, that complete uniformity can ever be obtained on all the roads of the United States. *Commodity tariffs*, peculiar and necessary to different localities, cannot perhaps with justice be abolished. Sometimes the classification of an article is not only arbitrary and unjust, but absolutely prohibitory of its transportation, and purposely made so. As in the case of railroad cross-ties, which many companies class so high as to prevent their shipment, and thus secure them for their own use, at prices which competition between purchasers can have no share in fixing.

"That the classifications now in use have been fairly arranged, with due regard to all the considerations which have been alluded to, cannot be justly claimed by the railroad authorities. In many instances it is difficult to ascertain the principles upon which they have been adjusted, or the reasons that originally dictated the marked differences that have often characterized the rates upon articles of a similar character. Differences have been preserved by custom, for which the original reason, if any existed, has been forgotten, with the result that they now appear arbitrary and unreasonable.

"The tariffs of the present day are a great advance upon those of a few years ago; but there is yet ample room for improvement. They have been a gradual growth, modified and improved from time to time as the principles which should govern their adjustment have become better understood, and as circumstances have seemed to make changes expedient, but they are yet too largely arbitrary."[1]

Besides the several methods by which railroad companies may discriminate as between individuals or localities, the same evil is sometimes produced by the existence of hostile relations between different companies, which result in an intentional failure to make proper connections, or to interchange traffic, on a just and equitable basis. The duties of the companies and the power of the public in the matter of a proper interchange of traffic have

---

[1] Report Cullom Committee, pp. 186, 187.

already been considered. No little inconvenience is sometimes experienced from the failure of connecting or intersecting roads to adjust their time-tables in the interest of travellers who wish to transfer from one road to the other. Where the reasonable accommodation of any considerable community, or any considerable volume of travel requires close connection to be made at intersecting or connecting points, and where such connection can be made with due regard for the necessity of making connections at other points, and without imposing unreasonable requirements upon the companies, they may certainly be compelled, in the interest of the public,—even if at some sacrifice of their own,—to make the proper connection.

Some writers upon the railway question, notably Mr. Edward Atkinson,[1] are so impressed with the contemplation of the enormous increase in national wealth, and the vast public benefits that have accrued from cheap transportation by rail, as to ignore or greatly belittle the evil that has been nourished and grown up with the good. And such persons deprecate any interference whatever with the business and the practices of the transportation companies. But that the railways have frequently used in an arbitrary and oppressive manner the great powers which their situation in the commercial world enables them to exercise over so many interests outside their own, is not to be denied; and the facility with which they may do so, and their temptations to perversion of

---

[1] See paper entitled "The Railway and the Farmer."

public duty, clearly show the necessity of subjecting their operations to special public supervision and regulation. They should no more object to proper public supervision than the national banks. Each performs a public function, and each should be subject to reasonable public regulation.

CHAPTER VII.

Methods Adopted or Proposed to Prevent Extortion and Unjust Discrimination—Publication of Rates—Statistical Reports—English "Railway and Canal Traffic Act"—Remedial Statutes Usually of Little Avail—The Commission System—Power to Fix Rates—To Revise Rates—To Hear and Decide Complaints—To Hear Complaints and Make Recommendations -- Examples — Georgia and Massachusetts—Theory of General Unrestricted Competition over the Same Line of Road Reviewed—Destructive of Commerce in Many Necessities of Life—Monopoly Essential to Public Interest—Theory of Public Ownership Reviewed—Would Fail to Prevent Discriminations.

EXTORTION and some kinds of discrimination are obnoxious to the principles of the common law, but there are other kinds for which it is doubtful if the common law provides, even theoretically, a remedy. And practically, in most cases, the disparity between the parties is so great where an individual undertakes to assert rights of this character against a railroad company that it is seldom attempted.[1] Accordingly provisions have frequently been incorporated into constitutions and statutes intended to deprive railroad companies, as far as possible,

---

[1] Note See R. R. Co. *vs.* Lockwood, 17 Wall, on p. 379.

of the power to perpetrate injustice on the public. And legislation has been enacted in many States, undertaking to define and expressly forbid extortion and unjust discrimination in the operation of railroads, and enlarging the remedies of the citizen against these practices.

Railroads are sometimes declared expressly to be public highways, though it is difficult to see how this mere declaration enlarges the power of the public over them. Consolidation and pooling by parallel or competing lines is sometimes prohibited, with the view of maintaining free competition. But the wisdom of the prohibition is doubtful when it is considered that the operation of competition is usually limited to a few localities, and that excessive competition in those localities tends to aggravate monopoly in localities where no competition exists.

In most jurisdictions, publication and conspicuous posting of rates, and of changes in rates, is required, and penalties are imposed for charging more or less than published rates. This provision is generally conceded to be one of the most effectual for the prevention of unjust discriminations, and of instability and sudden and unaccountable fluctuations in the prices of railroad transportation.

Steadiness and reasonable permanence in the prices of transportation services are among the chief essentials of success in any legitimate business, in which transportation by rail constitutes a considerable element.

Steady rates are far more desirable than much cheaper but more uncertain rates.[1] Every shipper has the right to know what the price of any given railway service will be to him, for it is one of the principal bases on which he contracts with his customers. And he also has the right to know what price is charged to his rival in business for the same or similar services, and to be protected against discriminations which put him at a relative disadvantage. By the better class of railroad managers publication of rates, and legal penalties for varying from them, seem to be earnestly desired.[2] Statutory prohibitions enable managers to refuse concessions which they do not desire to give, but which, under certain circumstances, it might otherwise be hard to refuse.

Statistical reports from railroad companies are required by nearly all States to be made to some public board or official. Throughout the United States there is considerable similarity in the forms of reports. But for the purposes of intelligent comparison of the data furnished by them respecting the condition and operation of roads in different sections and States, and of intelligent deductions from them, greater uniformity between the reports required in different jurisdictions is believed to be desirable. The discussions and resolutions in the recent conference of railroad commissioners in Washington, held under the auspices of the Interstate Commerce Commission, have

---

[1] See Mr. Russel's statement, Testimony, Cullom Committee, p. 300.
[2] Testimony, Cullom Committee, p. 1210.

initiated an organized movement in the direction of uniformity in our States. The form of report prescribed for carriers, subject to the Interstate Commerce Act, will doubtless soon be adopted in all the States. This goes with the fullest detail into the financial condition of all the companies, and into their entire field of operations. The history, organization, stock, funded and floating debt, cost of road and equipment, gross earnings, operating expenses, tonnage, ton mileage, average rate per ton per mile, passengers carried and passenger mileage, earnings from freight and passenger traffic separately, expenses allotted to each kind of traffic, subdivision of expenses to "maintenance of way," "maintenance of equipment," "conducting transportation," and "general expenses," as well as many other matters, are called for in the utmost detail. The mass of information thus furnished and tabulated is of the highest practical value.

In Pennsylvania, and in a number of other States, there is a constitutional provision that : " Every railroad company shall have the right with its road to intersect, connect with, or cross any other railroad, and shall receive and transport each the other's passengers, tonnage, and cars, loaded or empty, without delay or discrimination."

In some States, as in Massachusetts and Michigan, there are legislative enactments requiring connecting railroad companies to interchange traffic—transporting each the cars of the other on just and reasonable terms. And if the companies themselves cannot agree on the mode and terms of such interchange, the railroad commission, on notice to the parties, is authorized to fix the times and the terms upon which each company shall carry the vehicles and traffic of the other, in such manner as may be just between the companies, and for the interest and convenience of the public.

Provision is made for certifying the decision of the commission to the supreme judicial court, where it is "subject to revision in the same manner as if the board [of commissioners] had derived its powers in the premises under the appointment of said court."

The explicit terms of these provisions, which require and provide for enforcing a proper interchange of traffic in the public interest, have the effect to establish a "business connection" between the companies; and thus essentially differ from the constitutional provisions of Colorado, which were claimed to have the same effect, but which were interpreted by the United States Supreme Court as referring merely to a physical connection of tracks (see *ante* p. 14).

The provision against discriminations in the laws of many of the American States is based upon an act of the English Parliament, passed for the same purpose in the year 1854, styled the " Railway and Canal Traffic Act." This provided that no company should "make or give any undue or unreasonable preference or advantage to or in favor of any particular person or company, or any particular description of traffic, in any respect whatsoever," and should not "subject any particular person or company, or any particular description of traffic, to any undue or unreasonable prejudice or disadvantage, in any respect whatsoever." Another important provision of the English act, not usually found in the American laws, is that "every railroad company . . . working railways which form part of a continuous line of railway . . . communication, . . . shall afford all due and reasonable facilities for receiving and forwarding by one of such railways . . . all the traffic arriving by the others without any unreasonable delay and without any . . . preference or advantage, prejudice or disadvantage . . . and so that no obstruction may be offered to the public desirous of using such railways . . . as a continuous line of communication, and so that all reasonable accommodation may by means of the railways of the several companies be at all times afforded to the public in that behalf." This act as interpreted by the courts, says Mr. Sterne, "is one that, in the first place, prevents undue preferences, and, in the second place, compels interchange of traffic." But to remove doubts and ambiguities which seem to have arisen on this point, a very recent act of Parliament has explained and amended the provision last mentioned, by declaring that the facilities referred to therein shall include the due and reasonable receiving and forwarding of "through traffic" at "through rates" by connecting roads, at the request of either of the railroad companies, or at the request of any person interested in such traffic. Elaborate provision is made (in case a satisfactory arrangement can not be agreed on by the parties interested) for the designation of the through route and the establishment of a through rate and its apportionment among the different lines constituting the route, by the board of railroad commissioners.

The commissioners in discharging this function are directed to consider whether the "through route" and the "through rates" desired are due and reasonable facilities in the public interest.

Among other important provisions of recent English legislation may be mentioned the requirement that the classifications, and the schedules of maximum rates of railroad companies, shall be approved and adjusted by the Board of Trade, and submitted to Parliament for confirmation. Some degree of adaptability to changing conditions of traffic is provided for by giving the Board of Trade authority, upon application, after due publication of notice, to change, modify, or amend the classifications and tariffs.[1] According to Professor Hadley, who has carefully studied the railway systems of both this and foreign countries, in their relation to the public, the English railroad commissioners have construed the act of 1854 to mean that rates shall be based, to a very large extent at least, on cost of service; and have held that the

---

[1] English legislation, given in Second Annual Report (1888) of Interstate Commerce Commission.

existence of competition does not justify a departure from this rule; also that a greater charge must be made, and a greater net profit realized from the long haul than from the short haul, and that no more shall be charged for carrying a more valuable than a cheaper article of the same general character. And the regular courts at Westminster have decided that the act forbids charging less for the whole distance between any two points than for a part of that distance, thus extracting from the act the "long- and-short haul" principle, so much discussed in this country.[1]

The English courts, however, in construing the act, have admitted the principle of difference between wholesale and retail prices in trade, as applicable to transportation, and as justifying a lesser charge to the larger shipper, "provided the real object of the railway company be to obtain thereby a greater remunerative profit, by the diminished cost of carriage, although the effect may be to exclude from the lower rate those persons who cannot give such a guaranty."[2]

The Supreme Court of the United States has declared that the English cases "are instructive and of high authority as to what would be undue or unreasonable preference among competing customers" (110 U. S., p. 684). But the railroad commissions of our States have not generally given to similar enactments a construction

---

[1] "Railroad Transportation," pp. 182, *et seq.* and note.
[2] Nicholson *vs.* R. R. Co., 94th E. C. L. R., p. 440.

as broad as that which the English commissioners and courts have placed upon their law; and they have allowed discriminations in some cases—and apparently upon sound reasons—where their decisions would be repugnant to the English adjudications.

And even where legislation contains a specific provision on the subject of the long and short haul, it usually goes no further than to forbid a *greater* charge for the latter than for the former. As very justly observed by Mr. Hadley, the cost-of-service principle (which embraces the subject of the long and short haul) is generally used in America to prevent the creation of inequalities, while in England the same principle is used to prevent their abolition. Indeed State statutes, expressly forbidding a greater charge for the shorter than the longer transportation, have sometimes been violated by railroad companies with the tacit consent of the authorities, where their enforcement would manifestly have been unjust to the companies, and productive of no public good.[1] Besides the statutory prohibitions and requirements which have just been discussed, very summary and stringent remedies are usually provided for their violation, both by way of exemplary damages to the party injured thereby, and by way of fines in the nature of public punishment. But these provisions have been found insufficient to prevent the practices prohibited, or to put the parties on a footing of equality, at least as a general rule. Remedial laws

---

[1] See Interstate Com. Repts., vol. i., p. 141 (testimony).

of this kind, in fact, no matter how stringent, where their application is left solely to the individual action of the injured party, have usually been little more than dead letters. The reason of this is apparent. In the first place, the laws are frequently based upon false principles, whose practical application would be both unjust and injurious. In the second place, the amount involved in each case is frequently so small that the complainant cannot afford the expenses of litigation over it, while the principle involved is of such importance to the railroad companies that they are willing to incur large expense rather than suffer an adverse decision.

Some of the earlier Granger legislation, as it was commonly called, went the length of establishing directly by statute a system of railway tariffs, but this proved wholly impracticable, and was speedily abolished. Accordingly the commission system has now generally been adopted— that is, a special board charged with the duty of exercising over the transportation companies such powers as the State sees fit to delegate to it. Very different degrees of authority have been conferred upon railroad commissioners in different jurisdictions. In Georgia, for example, the commission is "authorized and required to *make* for each of the railroad companies doing business in this State . . . a schedule of just and reasonable *rates* and charges for the transportation of passengers and freights and cars over each of said railroads." But the Georgia law contains no specific provision on the subject of the long and short haul. In Alabama the commission is required to consider and carefully *revise* all *tariffs* of charges for transportation submitted to them by the railroad companies, and to notify the companies submitting the same of the changes, if any, deemed necessary to avoid extortion and unjust discrimination. The companies are, of course, required by the law to submit their tariffs to the commission for revision. In controversies upon the subject of rates, the revised tariffs are held to be *prima facie* right and just.

Certain discriminations are evidently contemplated by the Alabama law as reasonable and just, where they are necessary to enable the railroad company to make a fair net revenue on the just value of its property.[1] Probably the discriminations had in view were those arising from the comparative rates on long and short hauls, though the act contains no specific provision on that subject.

The "Interstate Law" of Congress is a good example of a still more limited degree of authority in the commission, which is, nevertheless, possessed of very large and useful powers, and which is to some extent directed to a particular course of action which is not prescribed in the States above referred to. The Federal law will be discussed in subsequent pages.

Finally the Massachusetts commission illustrates the class of commissions with the most limited powers, being

---

[1] See Section 6 of the Act of 1881.

merely those of *hearing complaints*, and making *recommendations* thereon.

The effect, and the mode of enforcing the decisions of railroad commissions varies in the different acts creating them. Usually their judgments, and the facts found by them, are directed to be held *prima facie* correct in all subsequent judicial proceedings. In no case, it is believed, in any State of the Union, have their judgments the finality and binding effect of those of a regularly constituted court, nor are they capable of being enforced by any process issuable by the commission itself. In this respect the powers of the American commissions fall short of those of the English commission, which is authorized to compel obedience to its orders by mandatory injunction.

In some States the commission having rendered its decision on any matter or question, is *functus officio*, and is not empowered even to apply to the courts to have the decision enforced. It therefore merely operates to place the party in whose favor it was rendered in a position of *prima facie* right in any subsequent litigation of the matter in court. And where criminal penalties are imposed on railroad companies for violations of duty, the finding of the commission, that the violation has occurred, is sometimes made *prima facie* evidence of guilt. Under some statutes the commission is authorized to apply to the proper court, at the costs of the State, for process to compel obedience to its decision or order; and in such cases, the action of the commission, though presumed to be right until otherwise shown, may on sufficient grounds be reversed.

In this way the constitutionality of the law, its interpretation, and its proper application to the evidence, may be brought before the regular judicial tribunals. The effect of a State investing corporations of other States with the right to operate its railways, as is frequently done by legislative acts authorizing or confirming consolidations and leases, is worthy of consideration in this connection. For the foreign corporation is entitled to transfer legal proceedings against it, of a civil nature, into the federal courts.[1] There are cases where the lessor company may be held liable for the torts of the lessee, and if the former is a domestic corporation, the State courts may retain jurisdiction over it. But the enforcement of a judgment can hardly, as a general rule, be as easy or satisfactory as it would be, if rendered against the operating company. And where proceedings of a civil nature are instituted to enforce the rights of individuals, or the orders of a State Commission in respect to reasonableness of charges, unjust discriminations, proper facilities for interchange of traffic, etc., it would seem that they must necessarily be against the operating company. And if so, though the subject-matter of litigation may be entirely within the jurisdiction of the State commission, and the State Court, yet the status

---

[1] R. R. Company *vs.* Kootz, 104 U. S., p. 5.

of the offending company as a foreign corporation entitles it to the judgment of the federal courts; and there the action of the State commission may be reviewed, and either affirmed or reversed.

It does not seem wise thus to commit the adjudication of the State's rights in the regulation of the domestic commerce upon its public highways to any other tribunals than its own.

The greater facility and cheapness with which commerce may be carried on over extensive railway systems as compared with the independent operation of connecting roads, and the consequent public benefit arising therefrom, should undoubtedly have great weight with a legislature in authorizing consolidations, purchases, and leases of connecting lines.

But it is highly desirable that the unification and consolidation of the railway transportation system, towards which the tendency is now so strong, should be accompanied with great legislative precaution, to prevent results such as have just been suggested as likely to follow. To meet these difficulties it is sometimes provided, in acts authorizing leases or sales of the works, property, and franchises of domestic corporations to foreign companies, or authorizing consolidations with such companies, that the latter "shall, for purposes of suing and being sued, be deemed domestic corporations." But the validity and effectiveness of such a proviso is very questionable. For it has been decided that where a railroad company of one State is operating railroads in another State, under a claim of authority from the latter, such company cannot, as a condition of continuing its business, be required to submit to the jurisdiction of the State courts, in litigation arising against it in the State. The right to the jurisdiction and judgment of a federal court is one which constitutionally belongs to the foreign corporation, and of which a State law cannot deprive it. (Barron *vs.* Burnside, 121 U. S., p. 186.) While therefore, the leasing of the railroads of one State to companies of another, certainly should be, and probably is, dependent on the will of the former State, yet if that State sanctions such a lease, it is very doubtful whether it can, even as a condition precedent, require that the lessee company shall be subject to the jurisdiction of its own courts.

A provision in the act authorizing such a lease, that "the lessee company shall, for the purposes of suing and being sued, be deemed a corporation of this State," would not in fact make it such a corporation, and probably would not oust the federal jurisdiction. To preserve the jurisdiction of the State courts, the corporation, which it is proposed to admit to the operation of railroads within the State, must in fact be made a corporation of the State. Where a consolidation of railroad companies of different States is contemplated, the identity of each within the limits of the State creating it may, by the use of apt language in the act of consolidation, be still preserved. And where this is done the consolidated company remains, as regards its operations in either of the States, a corporation of that State, and as such subject to the jurisdiction of its courts. (Muller *vs.* Dows, 94 U. S., p. 447; R. R. Co. *vs.* Whitton, 13 Wall 270; O. and M. R. R. Co. *vs.* Wheeler, 1 Black, 295.)

The same is true as regards a sale of railroad property to a corporation of another State, and there is no reason why it should not be true of leases also. In the case of Railroad Co. *vs.* Harris (12 Wall, 82), the Supreme Court said that it saw no " reason why one State may not make a corporation of another State, as there organized and conducted, a corporation of its own, *quo ad* any property within its territorial jurisdiction. . . . The question is always one of legislative intent, not of legislative power or legal possibility." In that case, however, it was held that the legislation of Virginia, permitting the B. and O. R. R. Co. to extend its road into that State, had not made the company, even within its limits, a corporation of Virginia. But in the case of Clarke *vs.* Barnard (108 U. S., 436), a Connecticut railroad company was authorized by the laws of that State, to purchase or lease railways in other States. The Connecticut company accordingly purchased a railroad in Rhode Island, belonging to a corporation of the latter State. This purchase was subsequently ratified and confirmed by the legislature of Rhode Island, by which body it was enacted, that the purchasing company " should have, use, exercise, and enjoy all the privileges and powers heretofore granted and belonging to " the selling company, "and be subject to all the duties and liabilities imposed upon the same by its charter and the general laws of the State." This language was held to make the purchasing company, in respect to its railroad in Rhode Island, a corporation in and of that State, for purposes of jurisdiction. Similar language should always be incorporated into legislative acts authorizing leases or sales of railroads to foreign corporations.

Where the power of fixing or revising railroad rates is vested in a commission, it is provided in perhaps all the statutes that the rates fixed shall be "just and reasonable," or that the revision of the tariff shall be so effected as to allow to the owners of the road a "fair and just return on the value of the railroad, its appurtenances and equipment." But whether the power lodged in the commission be that of primarily establishing rates, or that of revising tariffs already established by the companies, or that of hearing and deciding complaints of extortion and unjust discrimination, or that of merely hearing complaints and making recommendations,—in all these cases it is proper (and is sometimes expressly provided) that the commission should take into consideration the character and nature of the service to be performed, and the entire business and earnings of the railroad, with the view of allowing to the company a reasonable net return on the just value of its property. It has been shown that the just value of railway property is by no means synonymous with the amount of its capitalization, or even of its cost.

An enormous capitalization is sometimes referred to by railroad managers, in justification of charges that are complained of as exorbitant. Yet in point of fact the capitalization does not usually (except within narrow limits) affect the question of rates. Maximum rates by no means imply maximum revenues; the rates may be prohibitory. The object of managers is to secure maximum revenues, and with this end in view they adjust the tariffs whether the capitalization be large or small.

Even in States where practically absolute power over the rates of railways has been intrusted to the commission, as in Georgia for example, they have exempted from the operation of the long- and short-haul rule, roads which at the termini of the longer haul are compelled to meet competitors for traffic over whom the commission has no control. But questions of competition, distance, value of freight, and other circumstances have evidently entered into the basis upon which the Georgia commission has established tariffs for the railroads of that State, and greatly modified the cost-of-service principle, even where the competitors are all under the jurisdiction of the commission. As said by Major Campbell Wallace, the head of the Georgia commission, and a practical railroad man of very large experience : " A community having more railroads than one, or having one and a navigable water-course, has commercial and transportation advantages and facilities that, according to all the laws of trade and commerce, do not accrue to a community with only one railroad or simply a navigable watercourse."

And again Major Wallace, in his testimony before the Cullom Committee explaining the principles on which they fixed rates, said: " We take into consideration the length of the road, its grade, its curvature. We take into consideration the commerce that will naturally flow to it without competition or with competition. We do not interfere with any competing point, except that there is to be no discrimination."

Practically, the Georgia commission has found it necessary, it is said, to make numerous exceptions to the " standard tariff and classification " fixed by them, not only upon different roads, but on different articles of traffic on the same road ; and from time to time on the same commodities, as circumstances have shown to be necessary and just. This demonstrates the futility of attempting to establish permanent and unyielding rates of transportation by public authority. The Georgia commission has been one of the most successful of its class (*i. e.*, exercising such large powers), and it is claimed by its friends to have accomplished great public good in that State without detriment to the railway interests. Mr. Hadley suggests that its success in preventing discriminations has been not a little contributed to by the admirable pooling system of the Southern Railway and Steamship Association, of which most of the Georgia railroads are members. The fact seems to be that the Georgia commission always (and most wisely) confers freely with the railroad authorities in fixing schedules of rates, and allows variations from the "standard tariff," such as either general or special reasons show to be just. The commission's tariff, however, is by no means in all respects satisfactory to the railway interests.[1]

Turning now to the other extreme of the various theories of railway regulation by commissions,—namely, that of minimum powers,—as exemplified by its workings in the State of Massachusetts, it is said that all classes of the community, including both the railroads and the shippers, are perfectly satisfied with its results. The commission there has no power except to investigate complaints, to *recommend* to the railroad companies such action upon them as is deemed proper, and to report their proceedings and the conduct of the transportation companies to the legislature. Their findings of fact are not even *prima-facie* evidence in court (see Judge Russel's statement, Testimony, Cull. Com., p. 303), and their decisions have only such weight as may attach to their *intrinsic merit*. By the general law discriminations are forbidden, and no more is allowed to be charged for hauling the same class and quantity of freight a shorter than a longer distance *from the same original point of departure* and in the same direction. The long- and short-haul law, thus limited, is implicitly obeyed by the railroad companies, it is said, and they have almost invariably

---

[1] See vol. i., Interstate Com. Repts., p. 126 (testimony).

yielded to the recommendations of the commission, on whatever subject made—sometimes to their heavy pecuniary loss.[1]

One very beneficial result that has attended upon the labors of the Massachusetts commission, is the effect which their public hearing of complaints has had in removing erroneous impressions which people frequently entertain of injustice done them by the action of the railroads. The latter have in many instances been proven to the entire satisfaction of the complainants to be justifiable in pursuing the course complained of; and hence a better feeling between the different interests has resulted.

The Massachusetts system has been substantially adopted in New York—the more drastic measure recommended by the Hepburn Committee having been defeated,—and it is generally conceded to have produced excellent results. There are some States, however, where the commission with these limited powers has failed to accomplish much good, and the failure is usually attributed to its lack of authority.

But even where the commission is armed with very extensive powers, its workings have not always been by any means satisfactory; and the probability is that the success of both the Georgia and the Massachusetts commissions, organized as they are on such different theories, and with such different powers, has been more largely due

---

[1] See Testimony, Cull. Com., pp. 305, 306.

to the personal ability and fitness of their members for the discharge of the duties imposed on them, than to the character of the laws under which they have acted.

If this be true, it justifies, to a large extent at least, the remark of Mr. Adams, that a commission without any law is preferable to a law without the commission. But the correctness of this assertion depends on the material of which the commission is composed. Where the incumbent of such a position is elected upon political considerations, or those of personal popularity merely, without regard to fitness, it can only result in bringing the office into disrepute; and this has too often been the case. On the whole, however, the commission plan seems the best yet devised or suggested for the public regulation of railroad transportation. And that there should be a commission to represent the interest of the public in railroads and railroad transportation, results almost necessarily from the dual character of railroad property as already explained— that of *private ownership* clothed with a *public use*. It is certain that their owners and managers regard railroads chiefly from the proprietary standpoint, and operate them with a single eye to the private interests concerned. Nor should they be blamed for doing so. But as the managers serve primarily the private interests in the railroads, there should be public agents to serve the paramount public interests, not in the character of partisans, but to see that justice be done to all, so far as is practicable. The objection that the commissioners may fall under the influence of the corporations whose actions they are employed to supervise, is one that applies—though perhaps not always with the same force—to every public agency employed to represent the State, in dealing with parties whose interests are, or may be, antagonistic to those of the general public.

It applies to the post-office department, and the other departments of government in contracting for services and supplies, and it applies to the courts in the discharge of many of their duties. It has happened, unfortunately too frequently, that the public interests have been betrayed in these matters, either through corruption or favoritism. But the fact that a public office may be abused is no argument against its existence, when so many imperative reasons call for it. The vast preponderance of evidence is to the effect that the commission system, in many jurisdictions where it prevails, has greatly mitigated the evils of railway abuses where they really exist, and has often done scarcely less good in pointing out cases where methods and practices, commonly supposed to be unjustly discriminative, are not really obnoxious to that charge.

It should not be supposed, as without due consideration it sometimes is, that the mere presentation of a complaint to a railroad commission absolves the complainant from all further effort or participation in securing his rights. If the facts alleged by him are controverted, it behooves him, as a general rule, to prove them. But the commission is usually provided with powers to compel the production of testimony which to the complainant, unaided, would be practically inaccessible; and frequently, under an undisputed state of facts, a party may be entitled to relief which, without the commission's aid, he could never obtain. The proceedings before commissions, too, are attended with far less formality and technicality than are incident to proceedings in courts, and are not liable to delays from time to time, which, on one pretext or another, are so often resorted to by railway companies, until the hopes and the resources of the complainant are alike exhausted. The constitution of a railroad commission, which is supposed to be, and should be, composed of men of intelligence, versed in the matters which come before them, required to give their attention exclusively to the objects contemplated in the creation of their office, and prepared at all times to hear and decide complaints, is an immense aid in the administration of the law. To leave questions of the kind usually committed to a commission to an ordinary jury, drawn temporarily from a dozen different vocations, or to a court unfamiliar with the economic principles involved, taken up with controversies of a wholly different character, and limited to particular times and places for hearing causes, amounts to a practical denial of justice. By an intelligent and honest commission, such questions can be far more speedily and satisfactorily decided. And either party going into court with its favorable opinion would be very apt to prevail.

In a number of States, as in New York and Massachusetts, for example, the cost and expenses of the commission, including the commissioners' salaries, are assessed upon the railroads of the State, in proportion to their gross earnings, or on some other plan equitable to the companies. The constitutional power of the State to impose this expense on the companies regulated has already been somewhat discussed. But conceding the power to exist, the wisdom of its exercise is doubtful. For, while many persons will probably agree with Mr. Simon Sterne,[1] that it is not an imposition upon the companies to make them pay the cost of a tribunal which their peculiar conditions call into being, yet the companies themselves will sometimes (especially where the expense is considerable) consider it a very grievous and iniquitous imposition, and a strong feeling of antagonism is at once aroused.

Moreover, the public may be impressed with the idea that the commission is more or less robbed of its independence when its salaries come exclusively from the railroads, and are apt to attribute to this cause decisions which, however just, are favorable to the companies. Such a suspicion in the minds of the public, and such antagonism from the railways arising from a sense of injustice inflicted upon them, must detract greatly from the usefulness of any commission.

Evils and abuses, however, will probably always exist—

---

[1] See Testimony, Cull. Com., p. 80.

as they now do,—even under the most judicious system of governmental regulation. And this fact, together with the constantly growing tendency to railway consolidation, has recently elicited two propositions contemplating very radical changes in the operation of the railroad system, and illustrating an extreme divergence of theoretical views on the subject. One of these is the proposition to put in practice the old theory of railroad operation, and open transportation over every line of railroad to general competition. This suggestion is elaborated at great length by Mr. James F. Hudson in his able and interesting work, "The Railways and the Republic."

He would have a uniform rate of *toll* (in the proper sense of the word) prescribed by law for each road, to be paid, by parties using the road, to its owners. This toll to be a uniform rate per ton per mile on loaded cars, and a uniform rate per car per mile for empty cars, over the same road, regardless of distance, character of freight, or other circumstances. Mr. Hudson concedes, and elaborately attempts to refute, many of the objections to general competition which reflection will readily suggest—those, to wit, growing out of the public necessity of safety and celerity in railway transportation.

These objections he would obviate by giving to the railroad company proper very large powers in prescribing schedules, and rules and regulations for the running of trains over the road. But he does not seem to have considered the objection growing out of the public necessity for a classification of freight according to value, and the impossibility of maintaining such a classification under general competition and a system of uniform tolls. The two things certainly could not exist together. Competitors for traffic would, of course, seek the kind of business that affords profit—*i. e.*, articles that are classed high,—and the inevitable tendency of free competition would be to reduce charges to cost of service on all kinds of traffic. Having, therefore, no excess of profit on one class to compensate for absence of profit on other classes, the cheapest and most necessary articles of commerce could not be carried at all. For these, as has been shown, must necessarily be transported, if at all, at charges less than their ratable share would be if proportioned to cost of service. The classification might indeed be applied to the tolls instead of the traffic, but this would equally violate the theory of Mr. Hudson, who proposes complete uniformity of tolls.

The impossibility of fixing rates strictly in proportion to distance is so generally conceded, that it has not been discussed at any length in the foregoing pages; but it has been shown that the contrary practice, of charging less for longer than shorter distances, is, under some circumstances, highly essential to the public welfare. This would manifestly be impossible under general competition. Indeed, the object of Mr. Hudson would be, as avowed by him, to make it impossible. His theory is, that the public welfare requires that transportation charges should be based on cost of service alone, to which basis general competition would reduce them. But if the views heretofore advanced are sound, the public welfare would be very seriously disturbed by the application of the cost-of-service principle to railroad transportation, and hence general competition should never be permitted.

To maintain a classification based upon "what the traffic will bear," and to enable the transportation companies in certain cases to charge absolutely more, and in all cases to charge relatively more, for the shorter than the longer transportation, both of which things are frequently essential to the public good, a practically exclusive control over the traffic—and not merely over the time and manner of running trains,—a monopoly, in fact, would appear to be absolutely necessary.

Another proposition is that the government take full control of the operations of the railroad system, on its own account, just as it operates the postal department. It seems to be supposed by the advocates of this theory that discriminations in railway transportation would then cease.

The chief objection which has been suggested to the plan is the vast increase in governmental patronage, and consequent political corruption, which it would occasion. But leaving this consideration out of view, it is very doubtful if discriminations would cease. The railways can be acquired only by purchase or by the exercise of eminent domain, and either mode of acquisition involves the payment of a fair price for them. Indeed, it is quite doubtful whether they could be acquired by the federal government at all, without an amendment to the Constitution.

But suppose the government has the constitutional power to become the owner of the railroad system. It must first pay for the property.

Opinions vary greatly as to the just value of the railways of the country, with their equipment, but the best authorities estimate it at about $6,000,000,000—the capitalization being far in excess of this. The net earnings for several years past have averaged about $300,000,000, annually, while the expenses of maintenance, operation, etc., have usually been nearly double that amount. To become the owner of the railway system, then, assuming the income to represent its value—and taking the whole system as a unit, this would not be excessive,—the government would have to undertake the annual payment of about $300,000,000—to the present owners. The acquisition of the roads by the government would probably best be accomplished by issuing government bonds to be used in exchange for the outstanding railroad securities, at a proper valuation.

Thus a public debt of a magnitude never before approached would be created—say $6,000,000,000— at five per cent. Expenses of operation and maintenance being nearly double the amount of net earnings, the total amount to be annually raised by the government, to perform the railway transportation business of the country and pay the interest on the additional debt, would be about nine hundred million dollars. Of course it would be preposterous to think of supplying by general taxation any considerable deficiency in the revenues from transportation. The American people would never submit to it. The system would have to be not only self-sustaining, but at least profitable enough to pay the interest on the debt contracted for its purchase. The railroads then must be made to earn as much money under government ownership as they now do under private ownership. There is no doubt that the present system of discriminations is the means by which railroad earnings have been raised to their present figures. These discriminations, as has been shown, are sometimes unfortunate, but they are not necessarily unjust, while they are necessary to maintain revenues. Certain discriminations which the railways have endeavored to obviate by pooling would, no doubt, be more effectually checked under public ownership, the effect of which would indeed be to bring the whole railroad system under one vast pool.

But discriminations arising from water competition and from the comparative natural advantages of different rail routes would still exist, and it is difficult to see how government could abolish them without doing an injustice, which would never be tolerated, to sections of country enjoying superior natural advantages.

But apart from the foregoing considerations is that of the influence which, under government ownership, different sections of the Union, according to their various interests, would exert in the public management of the railroad system, and in the establishment of classifications, rates, traffic connections, etc., etc. The inevitable proneness of representative men to seek to promote the commercial interests of their immediate constituencies at the expense of other portions of the country, is constantly observable. It can hardly be doubted that under governmental ownership of railways there would be worked out, either by legislation or by departmental rules, a system of sectional discriminations worse than any which under private ownership can possibly be imposed.

Government probably would not fall into the error of building unnecessary lines of road, and this would be an undoubted advantage of public ownership. But, on the other hand, it is likely that the development of new territory would be seriously retarded by the refusal of government to extend the railway system, except under circumstances likely to make the extension immediately remunerative, or at least self-sustaining.

CHAPTER VIII.

THE INTERSTATE COMMERCE ACT.

Analysis of the Act—Powers of Commission—Decisions concerning Long and Short Haul—Discriminations between Places, Persons, and Kinds of Traffic—Effects of the Act—Tendency toward Combination—A Railway " Trust."

THE legislation recently enacted by Congress for the regulation of commerce by railway is the result of more careful and intelligent deliberation perhaps than any other measure of similar character, and it is not unlikely that the legislation of many of the States will sooner or later be conformed to it. The general provisions intended to prevent extortion and unjust discrimination are not unlike those which have already been discussed. The powers conferred by the act upon the commissioners are in a certain sense judicial, inasmuch as they are authorized to hear and decide complaints of violations of the law. Yet their decisions lack the finality and binding effect of the judgments of a court, and are not enforcible by any process issuable by the commission itself. The enforcement of their decisions is left to the regular courts, where the conclusions and findings of fact of the commission, though held to be *prima facie* correct, may on sufficient grounds be reversed. To have conferred strictly judicial powers on the federal commission would have been to make of it a court, of which the members under the constitution hold office for life, and not for a mere term of years. Its functions are, perhaps, as nearly judicial as could be made, without conferring a life tenure upon its members. The powers of the commission in administering the law are also limited by analogy to those of the regular courts; inasmuch as they cannot decide upon hypothetical or *ex-parte* statements of cases, but only upon complaints of actual infraction of the law duly presented and verified. Considerable verbiage is used in the act of Congress to define and limit the subjects to which it is intended to apply, and the attempt at too much detail in specification may give room for construction which will rob the measure of some of its desired effect; that is, if its object was, as commonly supposed, the regulation of all such commerce carried on by railroads as Congress is empowered to regulate.

The provisions of the act apply to common carriers engaged in transportation "wholly by railroad, or partly by railroad and partly by water, when both are used, under a common control, management, or arrangement, for a continuous carriage" from State to State, etc.

This language confines the scope of the law within much narrower limits than might, under the authority of the Constitution, have been fixed; for it exempts from its operation commerce carried on by two independent agencies, one of which operates by water; and it contemplates, apparently, a continuous carriage from State to State, etc. And although Section 7 of the act is intended to prevent evasions of its purpose by any breach in the continuity of the carriage *made intentionally to evade it*, yet it seems probable that the terms of the law fail to cover some very important cases of interstate commerce carried on by rail. The provisions of the act apply to both passenger and freight transportation. All charges made for or in connection with transportation services, or for receiving, storing, handling, and delivering freight, are required to be "just and reasonable," and "every unjust and unreasonable charge for such service is prohibited and declared to be unlawful." On the general subject of discriminations it is declared to be unlawful, for any common carrier subject to the provisions of the act, "to make or give any undue or unreasonable preference or advantage to any particular person, company, firm, corporation, or locality, or any particular description of traffic, in any respect whatsoever, or to subject any particular person, firm, company, corporation, or locality, or any particular description of traffic, to any undue or unreasonable prejudice or disadvantage, in any respect whatsoever."

It is also provided that "every common carrier subject to the provisions of this act shall, according to their respective powers, afford all reasonable, proper, and equal facilities for the interchange of traffic between their respective lines, and for the receiving, forwarding, and delivering of passengers and property, to and from their several lines, and those connecting therewith, and shall not discriminate in their rates and charges between such connecting lines ; but this shall not be construed as requiring any such common carrier to give the use of its tracks or terminal facilities to another carrier engaged in like business." The expression " interchange of traffic," used in this connection, generally conveys the idea of a railway company hauling the cars of connecting lines over its track without breaking bulk or transferring the contents of loaded cars from the vehicles of one company to those of the other. But it can hardly be said that such a meaning is so well settled as to make it certain that the courts will give that construction to the language. This effect was probably intended, but it would have been prudent to use more explicit terms ; for, as has been previously pointed out, the Supreme Court has decided that language merely forbidding discrimination, and requiring equal facilities to be given, will not authorize the courts to compel a railroad company to make joint through-traffic arrangements with all connecting roads, merely because it chooses to make such arrangements by contract with one or more particular roads. The English " Railway and Canal Traffic Act " has been construed to have the effect of preventing discrimination of that kind, although the expression "interchange of traffic" is not used in it. But the act of Congress departs from the terms of the English law in this particular, and it would be hazardous to attempt any forecast of the construction which will be given it. Any thing like general competition over the same line of railway is of course precluded by the provision that no company "shall be required to give the use of its tracks and terminal facilities to another carrier engaged in like business." The language forbidding discriminations between persons, localities, and descriptions of traffic, it will be observed, is identical with that of the English provision on the same subject, which has been construed as requiring charges to be based in large measure on cost of service alone. But the general spirit of the federal law manifestly contemplates that other considerations besides mere cost of service should enter into the charges of railways, and will preclude the commission and the courts from giving such a construction to the language. In addition to the general anti-discrimination clauses above quoted, the act contains one provision directed specifically against personal discriminations, and another against one class of local discriminations. And both these provisions contain limiting clauses of very great importance, upon which widely different constructions were placed in the discussions of the measure in the houses of Congress. By the first of these provisions, common carriers subject to the operation of the act are forbidden to charge more to one person than another for "a like and contemporaneous service in the transportation of a like kind of traffic *under substantially similar circumstances and conditions*," and any evasion of this provision by special rate, rebate, drawback, or other device is prohibited. By the other provision it is made "unlawful, for any common carrier subject to the provisions of this act, to charge or receive any greater compensation in the aggregate for the transportation of passengers, or of like kind of property, *under substantially similar circumstances and conditions*, for a shorter than for a longer distance over the same line in the same direction, the shorter being included within the longer distance."

But upon application to the commission provided for by the act, "such common carrier may in special cases, after investigation by the commission, be authorized to charge less for longer than for shorter distances, for the transportation of passengers or property; and the commission may from time to time prescribe the extent to which such designated common carrier may be relieved from the operation of this" rule.

The "*circumstances and conditions*" which appear to justify a lesser charge for the longer haul have already been discussed, and if the conclusions arrived at are sound, the cases which should be excepted from the long- and short-haul rule are very numerous and very important.

Agreements "for the pooling of freights of different

and competing railroads, or to divide between them the aggregate or net proceeds of the earnings of such railroads," are prohibited, and each day of the continuance of a pooling agreement is made a separate offence. Some observations on the methods, objects, and results of pooling have already been submitted. The object, of course, is to maintain rates, and the division of earnings is resorted to as the means of enforcing the agreement to maintain rates. The federal law does not prohibit agreements for this purpose, but is only directed against one of the means—(that of pooling)—which has been devised to uphold such agreements. Every carrier subject to the act is required to print and post for public inspection at its depots and stations, schedules of the passenger and freight rates " in force at the time upon its route." And "the schedules printed as aforesaid by any such common carrier shall plainly state the places upon its railroad between which property and passengers will be carried, and shall contain the classification of freight in force, and shall also state separately the terminal charges, and any rules or regulations which in any wise change, affect, or determine any part or the aggregate " of charges made.

No advance in the rates so published and posted can be made except after ten days public notice, and no reduction except after three days public notice. To charge more or less than schedule rates is specifically forbidden, and declared to be unlawful. Copies of the schedules of rates are to be filed with the commission, who are also to be promptly notified of any changes made in the schedules.

"Every such common carrier shall also file with said commission copies of all contracts, agreements, or arrangements with other common carriers in relation to any traffic affected by the provisions of this act, to which it may be a party. And in cases where passengers and freight pass over continuous lines or routes operated by more than one common carrier, and the several common carriers operating such lines or routes establish joint tariffs of rates or fares or charges for such continuous lines or routes, copies of such joint tariffs shall also in like manner be filed with said commission." Advances in joint rates can only be made after ten days' notice to the commission, and reductions in them only after three days' notice to the commission. Variations from the joint tariffs as filed with the commission are also expressly forbidden and declared to be unlawful. These *joint* tariffs, as well as changes in joint rates, are to be made public when and to the extent directed by the commission; being thus put by the law on quite a different footing, as regards publicity at least, from the tariffs of a single road under one control and management. The latter, and all changes in them, are imperatively required to be made public, the commission having no discretion on the subject. Ample provision is made for the enforcement, by the federal courts, of the law requiring publicity of tariffs. By the above outlined provisions, extortion and unjust discrimination in railroad management are sought to be prohibited. Violations of the law may be visited with criminal penalties in the federal courts, and any person damaged thereby may sue in those courts for the recovery of such damages and costs, including a reasonable attorney's fee. Underbilling and false classification of freight, both by the carrier and its officers who permit it, and by the shipper who practises it, are made misdemeanors punishable by fine and imprisonment, as is also the securing of unjust advantages in transportation by improper solicitation or bribery. One of the most important provisions of the law is that of creating a commission and defining its powers. This body consists of five members appointed by the President and confirmed by the Senate, who are authorized and required to execute and enforce the provisions of the law, acting for this purpose through the proper law officers of the United States, and at the cost of the government. They are also required to keep themselves informed as to the business of all carriers subject to the act, and are empowered to obtain all the information necessary for the discharge of their duties. For this purpose they are authorized to examine witnesses, and to require the production of the books, papers, contracts, etc., of railroad companies; and the attendance of witnesses and production of papers may be compelled by the courts if necessary. On complaint made by any person, association, etc., or forwarded by the railroad commission of any State, they shall notify the company complained of to satisfy the complaint or answer the same in writing within a reasonable specified time. Unless the complaint is satisfied the commission must investigate it, if there are reasonable grounds for doing so (or it may of its own motion without complaint investigate any matter); and must make a report on the investigation, which shall include both the findings of fact and the recommendations of the commission. Such findings of fact are to be held *prima facie* correct and true in all subsequent judicial proceedings. Where the conclusion of the commission is against the railroad company, the latter shall be served with a copy of the report, and notified to cease from violation of the law, within a reasonable specified time. If the carrier neglects or refuses to obey the order of the commission, it shall be lawful for the commission, or for any person interested in the order, to apply to the federal courts for an injunction to restrain the further violation of the law, or to enforce compliance with the orders of the commission. In this way the matter comes for hearing before the regular courts, where the action of the commission may be either affirmed or reversed. Obedience to the injunction of the court—where the action of the commission is affirmed—may be enforced by pecuniary penalties payable to the complainant, or otherwise as the court may direct; and this penalty may be imposed on officers of the railroad, as well as on the company itself. When such an application to the courts is made by the commission, it shall be through the district attorney, and at the cost of the United States. And for the purpose of making all needful decrees and orders, in the matter of such applications, the courts shall be deemed to be always in session. Any party may appear and be heard before the commission in person or by attorney, and its proceedings shall be public upon the request of any person interested. The commissioners are authorized to require every railroad company subject to their jurisdiction, to make an annual report containing a complete exhibit of its operations and finances, rates, traffic agreements, contracts with other carriers, etc., etc. They are required to make an annual report of their own work to Congress, together with such information, recommendations, and data, as they may deem necessary.

It was of course, to be expected that any measure introduced into Congress, to place the vast railway interests of the country under legal restraints and public supervision, would encounter strenuous opposition. The debates in the two houses during the session of 1886–7 furnish ample illustration. The principal controversies arose over the question of pooling, and of the long and short haul. The result as to pooling was the provision totally forbidding the practice. In the case of the long and short haul, the result was the adoption of the clause limiting the prohibition to charge more for the latter than the former, to cases where the circumstances and conditions are substantially similar, with a proviso that this should not be construed as allowing as great a charge for the short as for the long haul.

When the law first went into effect frequent applications were made by the railroads to the commissioners for their opinion as to what circumstances and conditions would justify the greater charge for the shorter transportation. Many companies sought upon their own statement of the circumstances and conditions surrounding their business, to elicit an opinion as to their rights, in advance of any complaint against them of infraction of the law.

The commissioners very properly invariably refused to forestall their conclusions in this way, declaring that the railroad companies must in the first instance decide for themselves what circumstances and conditions will justify a departure from the general rule.

Certain general principles, however, were early announced by the commission as a guide to the carriers in their operations under this section of the act.[1] The phrase "under substantially similar circumstances and conditions," in the long- and short-haul clause, is declared to have the same meaning as it has in the section forbidding personal discriminations. The burden of proving a dissimilarity of circumstances, etc., is on the carrier who violates the general rule. Charges must be reasonable, and unjust discriminations are forbidden, even where the

---

[1] See Report Interstate Commission, 1887, p. 84, and 1st Interstate Commerce Reports, p. 278. (The Louisville and Nashville case.)

general rule may be lawfully departed from. It is not a sufficient justification for a departure from the general rule, that the traffic which is subjected to the greater charge is *way* or local traffic, while that which receives the more favorable rates is not; nor that the short-haul traffic is more expensive, unless the greater expense is exceptional and susceptible of definite proof; nor that the motive of the lesser charge for the longer haul is the encouragement of manufactures; nor that it is designed to build up business or trade centres.

" The fact," says the commission, " that long-haul traffic will only bear certain rates is no reason for carrying it at less than cost at the expense of other traffic." In reference to what will justify a departure from the general rule, the commission says: " That the existence of actual competition, which is of controlling force in respect to traffic important in amount, may make out the dissimilar circumstances and conditions entitling the carrier to charge less for the longer than the shorter haul, over the same line in the same direction, the shorter being included in the longer, in the following cases: 1. When the competition is with carriers by water which are not subject to the provisions of the statute. 2. When the competition is with foreign or other railroads which are not subject to the provisions of the statute. 3. In rare and peculiar cases of competition between railroads which are subject to the statute, when a strict application of the general rule of the statute would be destructive of competition."

It will be observed that the commission declares the existence of competition to justify a greater charge for the shorter haul; but confines it, where the competing roads are all subject to the act, to "rare and peculiar cases. . . . when a strict application of the general rule would be destructive of competition." This is a somewhat narrower application of the principle of exception to the general rule of the long and short haul, than that which has been suggested as the correct one in the preceding pages. The maintenance of competition seems to be the only object had in view by the commission in allowing the exception. But it has been shown that while the *existence* of competition is the sole justification of departure from the general rule, the *maintenance* of that principle is by no means the only public benefit that may result therefrom. It is quite conceivable, and probably frequently happens, that competition may be maintained without any departure from the general rule. There may be several competitors, a few of whom may be so fortunately circumstanced that they can comply with the general rule and still prosper. These few may maintain the competition. The other competitors may be weak lines which, by reason of the relatively small volume of their local traffic, or otherwise, must take the competitive traffic, if at all, under the exception to the general rule. They may do this and still derive an *increment of profit* from it, which enures to the benefit of the local communities which they serve. This certainly is a public benefit—not, indeed, arising from competition, but from a diffusion and partial equalizing of commercial advantages between different sections as has been heretofore explained. The stronger competing lines in the case supposed would probably complain of the competition of the weaker line as "illegitimate"; and under some circumstances doubtless it might be so. But the illegitimacy would seem frequently to consist only in diverting a portion of the profits the former might make into the treasury of the latter, while the general public good would undoubtedly be promoted.

The commission, while construing the fourth section of the act (the long- and short-haul section) to restrict their powers in this regard, are evidently of opinion that its enforcement under their construction may sometimes be inequitable, and prejudicial to the interests even of the local traffic. This appears from the opinion in the case of the Boston & Albany R. R. Co. *vs.* The Boston & Lowell R. R. and other companies (Interstate Com. Repts., vol. i., p. 571). In that case an association composed of the Boston & Lowell and other roads, forming with it a line from Boston through Massachusetts, New Hampshire, Vermont, and Canada, to Montreal, Detroit, and Chicago, under the name of the National Dispatch Line, *joined in fixing rates* from Boston to the points named.

And the rates fixed from Boston to those points were less than the rates charged over a portion of the roads composing the Dispatch Line from Boston to St. Albans, Vermont, an intermediate point.

The commission considered the word "line" in the fourth section to refer to a physical line, not a business connection. And they had "no difficulty in holding that if the defendants join in making the tariff which constitutes the lesser charge on the longer haul, while one or more of their number make the greater charge on the shorter haul, the case is within the fourth section, and those who make such greater charge are called upon to justify it."

Justification was sought to be established on the ground of competition which existed at Montreal, Detroit, and Chicago, but not at St. Albans, and there was strong evidence to show that rates on the through traffic could not be materially advanced without losing it, and that such traffic at existing rates added largely to net earnings. Also that the companies could not afford to reduce rates on local traffic.

The commission declared itself "entirely satisfied that a large through business is essential to this line, if it is to continue to be a useful line even for local business." It was also said that "no injustice is done to the local traffic by taking through traffic at very low rates, provided the doing so neither makes the local traffic more expensive, nor otherwise incommodes it." And it was plainly intimated that "a board having full power to adjust rates as circumstances should seem to require," might hold differently from the commission acting under the positive mandates of a statute. But it being established by the evidence that the competition which affected the action of the defendant roads was that of the trunk lines, all of which were under the jurisdiction of the commission, it was held that the "circumstances and conditions" justifying a greater charge for the shorter haul were not established, and the defendants were ordered to desist from the practice.

One of the most important decisions of the commission is that rendered "in the matter of the Chicago, St. Paul & Kansas City R. R. Co." (to be reported in 2d Interstate Com. Repts.). The company named having been compelled by the action of competing lines, and in conformity with the requirements of the long- and short-haul law, to make repeated changes in its tariff within a brief period of time, finally notified the commission of its intention to adopt a tariff by which a lesser charge would be made between Chicago and St. Paul than between Chicago and intermediate places.

Being cited before the commission to justify this action if possible, the company attempted to do so by showing that a rival in the Chicago-St. Paul business had reduced its rates to figures that failed to pay operating expenses, and that the same fate threatened its own revenues unless it should be allowed to meet the rival's rates at terminal points without making corresponding reductions at intermediate places. It was clearly pointed out that the "additional expense" of the competitive traffic was small, even compared with the excessively low charges upon it, and it was shown with equal clearness that a general reduction of charges in conformity with the long- and short-haul rule would result in serious financial disaster. It was insisted that the uncontrolled action of a rival road in fixing transportation charges at figures unreasonably low, should be held to constitute a case of dissimilar circumstances and conditions, justifying a greater charge on a shorter haul. Finally, it was forcibly urged that such action on the part of a road within the jurisdiction of the commission was subject to the control of the commission, and that the section of the law requiring all railroad charges to be reasonable and just, and forbidding all unjust and unreasonable charges, "prohibits and makes unlawful a rate or charge which is *too low*, as well as a rate or charge which is *too high* to be just and reasonable." Seeing that the commission had in several instances actually specified and fixed rates which in its opinion would be just and reasonable—although no power to fix charges was expressly conferred by the interstate law,—the position here taken by the railroad company as to the powers of the commission does not seem wholly unsupported. And indeed it was said in the opinion: "Possibly if the statute were to be interpreted without any aid from its history, and with no other knowledge of its purposes, aims, and ends, than such as may be derived from its provisions, a holding that a rate unreasonably low was forbidden might be justified, or at least might be urged upon plausible arguments. "But every statute is to be read in the light of its history and of the evils it was intended to redress. And as matter of public history nothing can be more notorious than that the act to regulate commerce had for its leading and general purpose, to which other purposes were subordinate, to provide effectual securities that the general public in making use of the means of railroad transportation provided by law for their service, should have the benefits which the law had undertaken to give, but of which in very many cases it was found the parties entitled to them were deprived by the arbitrary conduct, the favoritism, or the unreasonable exactions of those who managed them. It may be affirmed with entire confidence that the act was not passed to protect railroad corporations against the misconduct or the mistakes of their officers, or even primarily to protect such corporations against each other." The terms "just and reasonable" in the statute "were employed to establish a maximum limitation for the protection of the public; not a minimum limitation for the protection of reckless carriers against their own action. . . . But we cannot agree that because the commission has no authority to require a carrier to increase the rates it has voluntarily established on its line, the competition of carriers who come under the act to regulate commerce is subject to no more restraint than is that of others. It may perhaps be subject to no restraint directly applied; but many of the requirements of the act must have an important restraining influence." And having referred to several provisions of the interstate commerce law tending to restrain undue competition, the commission further remarked: "It may be quite true as respondent contends, that unless other carriers are suffered to meet the competition of a rival at an important point, without reducing intermediate rates, they will suffer unreasonably, perhaps destructively, in their resources. But this question is not to be decided on the interest of the carriers only; the communities which the act undertakes to protect are to be regarded also. The act has doubtless conferred upon the commission a greater power to protect localities against the carriers, than it has to protect the carriers against themselves, or against each other. It was probably thought in Congress that with the liberty of action left to the carriers, they would not needlessly rush to destruction. The assumption may not prove to be well founded; but nothing seems plainer than, that under the law as it stands, the protection of carriers against destructive rivalry, and rates that lead directly to bankruptcy, must be found chiefly in prudent management, in the cultivation of reasonable relations among themselves, in mutual forbearance, and the application of a sense of justice to their mutual dealings and in their rivalries. If they deliberately proceed to destroy each other, the law must take care that in doing so they injure as little as possible individuals and communities dependent upon them for transportation facilities." The decision of the commission that it has no power to protect the carriers against the excessive and unjust competition of rivals, is, no doubt, a proper interpretation of the intent of the framers of the "act to regulate commerce." But its action must frequently be harsh and inequitable. To the unprejudiced student of the transportation question nothing is more apparent than that uncontrolled competition between rival carriers is one of the great underlying causes of the outrageous personal and local discriminations in railroad charges which resulted in the enactment of the Interstate Commerce Law. And this decision demonstrates the great inherent defect of that measure, which seeks to cure the disease, but forbids the forcible removal of the cause of the malady; which contents itself with the application of local remedies to the various external manifestations of disorder, but fails to strike at the organic trouble which vitiates the system. When unembarrassed by the stringent statutory requirement in respect to the long and short haul, and guided only by the rule of "reasonable and just," operating between the carrier and its patrons, the commission has been able to put its judgments upon a basis which better commends them to the unbiased investigator of these questions.

It has been repeatedly decided, for example, that equal rates per ton per mile, for long and for short distances on the same road, are not required by this rule; nor is it "reasonable and just," within the meaning of the law, that a railroad company should be compelled to accept as the price of transportation of freight originating and ending at the respective termini of its own road, the share which the company receives of a joint rate on the same freight transported in part over other lines as well as its own.

In fact it is not always "unjust or unreasonable" to make the same charge for an appreciably different service in respect of the same kind and quantity of freight,—as where localities unequally distant from a common market are given the same rate to that market on certain commodities. No producer or shipper has an exclusive right to supply a market, and the interest of consumers, and of the public generally, may justify carriers in enlarging the field from which the demand for a commodity may be supplied, on terms of equality for transportation. But where the demand is limited, the extension of equal rates to more distant points of production may operate to produce an undue prejudice or disadvantage.

In all cases this practice must be restrained within reasonable limits; and the question whether an unjust discrimination is occasioned by it is principally one of fact, and not solely of law.[1]

In the Danville case (1 Inter. Com. Rept. 703) the

---

[1] See case of "Group-Rates" on coal, decided by commission, March 25, 1889.

complaint was of unjust discrimination against Danville, in the charges of the Richmond & Danville R. R. Co., especially in favor of the cities of Richmond and Lynchburg. The city of Danville is located at the intersection of the main line of the R. & D. R. R. with its Richmond branch. The N. & W. R.R. intersects the main line at Lynchburg, 65 miles north of Danville, and the C. & O. R. R. intersects the Richmond branch at Richmond, 140 miles N. E. of Danville. Freights were consigned from and to Danville, to and from the west and northwest, on through bills of lading over the Richmond and Danville road, and its connections at Richmond and Lynchburg. And it was proven that the rate, on grain for instance, from Chicago to Lynchburg, a distance of 800 or 900 miles, was 22 cents per cwt., while the rate to Danville, only 65 miles further on, was 34 cents per cwt.; and the differences on flour, meats, and other provisions were shown to be in like proportion. The same differences in charges were made from Danville, and from Richmond and Lynchburg respectively, to the west and northwest; it being alleged, for example, that while the rate on tobacco from Richmond to San Francisco was from $1.50 to $1.60 per cwt., the rate from Danville *via* Richmond to San Francisco, on through bills issued by the Richmond & Danville R. R., was $3. The people of Danville, conceiving the existence of this state of things to be an outrageous discrimination against them, applied to the Interstate Commerce Commission for relief.

The R. & D. R. R. Co., however, denied all responsibility for rates between Danville and points not on its own line, except for so much of the transit as was over its own line. In other words the R. & D. Co., while issuing through bills by arrangement with its connecting roads, for the accommodation of shippers, did not join with its connections in making rates. It charged its regular local rates for so much of the carriage as was over its own line, and did not pro-rate charges with its connections. And it maintained that these local rates were no more than reasonable and just, though they were out of all proportion to rates charged by connecting roads on the same traffic to Richmond and Lynchburg. "This," said the commission "is undoubtedly a great hardship to the Danville dealer, who must not only pay more freight moneys than his competitor would pay on a like consignment, but more in proportion to the distance the property is transported." The local rates are so much higher than the rates charged on the through lines, that the commission declared it was " not surprising that one who compares them without making inquiry into the circumstances under which the charges respectively are made, is inclined to pronounce the charges of defendant unfair and excessive." "The Richmond and Lynchburg dealer, therefore, acquires his stock at a less cost than does the dealer at Danville, and is able to undersell the latter almost at his own doors." "It is very evident from the testimony that the hardships of which the witnesses complain, arise chiefly from the great disparity between the local and through rates."

Two assumptions, the commission said, were made by the complainants. " The first is that defendant may be held responsible for the rates made on connecting lines, when through rates are named to consignors over such lines, in connection with its own; and the second is that rates made on long through lines may form a just basis of comparison with defendant's rates, when the reasonableness of the latter is in question." That defendant " is responsible for the local rates is unquestionable, for it makes those without the concurrence or interference of any other carrier —at least so far as any evidence before us shows. Perhaps it is not unnatural that a customer of the road, who did not inquire into the facts, should suppose the defendant to be in some measure responsible for the through rates also, especially if he found that defendant issued through bills over its own and other lines, named the through rates to those who asked for them, and received payment of freight moneys for the whole distance, exactly as it would if the whole amount were its own. All these things may happen and still the defendant not be responsible for the making of any rate off its own line. In most respects carriers by railroad may act independently, provided they afford to each other all proper facilities for the interchange of traffic. It is for this reason that railroad controversies, and questions of rates are attended by so many special embarrassments; they cannot be adjusted as they might be if all roads belonged to one system and were under a single control. If that were the case the rates might be so arranged as to prevent many of the inequalities that are now liable to operate oppressively to particular localities. When intersecting roads are separately controlled and owned, it may well happen that one which is of the very highest importance to the community it serves, and which deals with them fairly, shall nevertheless be powerless to prevent the rates of other roads giving to some of its towns great advantages over others, unless it consents to sacrifice its own revenues in doing so. Possibly this may be the case here. . . . The difference between the local and through rates is certainly very marked and striking, and it results unfavorably to Danville because Richmond and Lynchburg, which are competing towns for the trade along the line of defendant's road, are directly upon the long through lines, while Danville is not. . . . For this good fortune the defendant is not to be thanked by the favored towns, or blamed by the other. The obligation of defendant is to make rates on its own line, which are fair, reasonable, and undiscriminating; and if it does this the responsibility, if there is any, for inequalities as between towns on its line, which result from the rates made by other carriers, must rest upon those who make them."

Having thus shown the error of the first assumption made by the complainants, namely, that the defendant road was responsible for rates made on connecting lines, the commission proceeded to examine the other assumption, and "to consider whether the rates charged on defendant's road are shown, by comparison made with rates on other lines, to be excessive and unreasonable." "In the main the comparison has been made by the witnesses with rates on through lines over which the great bulk of the traffic in grain, flour, dressed and canned meats, and provisions passes from interior points to the seaboard. The difference between the rates charged for transportation over those lines and the rates made by the defendant is so very great that some of the witnesses in testifying have not hesitated to declare that defendant's charges were thereby proved to be excessive. The logic which brings the mind to this conclusion is that other roads would not accept the low rates unless they were profitable, and if profitable to them, rates made by defendant, which are several times as high, must necessarily be exorbitant. This logic, unfortunately, though at first blush it seems reasonable, does not always stand the test of examination.

"It is a well-known fact in transportation, that the cost of carriage depends very largely upon the volume of business, the cost of carrying five tons being very much greater in proportion than the cost of carrying a thousand tons over the same line. That carrier, therefore, can give the best rates whose business is the largest and most steady ; and as the through lines between the Mississippi and the seaboard are the best situated for a large and steady business, they can undoubtedly, as a general fact, give much better rates than the roads which intersect them ; but it is equally well known that the proportionate cost is diminished with the increase of distance, and as the through lines carry the traffic mentioned a very long distance before delivering to defendant the proportion which is to go over its road, they are, for this additional reason, enabled to make exceptionally low rates. These two facts are quite sufficient to render any comparison between the rates charged by the leading through lines and those made by the defendant of little or no value. The circumstances and conditions under which the traffic is carried by the through and the intersecting roads, respectively, are too great and too diverse to admit of useful comparison. . . . The comparison, if made at all, should be with local rates. Even then, it would not be very conclusive, without an inquiry into the conditions and circumstances of the traffic on the roads whose rates were compared, for freights on some roads, for a diversity of reasons which it is needless to undertake to specify here, can be carried much more cheaply than on others. . . . We are constrained to say, therefore, that the rates charged by the defendant, and which the petitioners complain of as excessive, are not shown by the proofs to be so."

In the case just commented on, it was decided that the railroad company might impose its usual local charges between Danville and Lynchburg on freight consigned on "through bills" from Danville via Lynchburg to the West. The power of the commission to compel connecting railway companies to unite in making joint through rates, on a pro-rating basis, was not directly involved. Subsequently, in the case of Bridge Co. *vs.* Railroad Co. (2 Int. Com. Repts.), the commission, on complaint of the bridge company (holding it under the facts of the case to be a common carrier subject to the act), ordered the railroad company to "afford all reasonable, proper, and equal facilities for the interchange of traffic between the respective lines of the parties, and for receiving, forwarding, and delivering of property to and from their respective lines and those connecting therewith." This order did not undertake to fix the terms or the details of interchange between the parties, and the question of "through rates" was not passed upon. In a suit brought by the bridge company in the federal court to compel the railroad company to obey the order of the commission, the court reversed the commission's decision. Very recently the commission has held that, although Congress probably intended that connecting roads should be compellable to make through routes and give through rates to the public, yet existing legislation does not clothe the commission with authority to decide upon and enforce the details necessary to a joint "through business," such as the establishment and apportionment of a rate. Further legislation to this end was therefore recommended to Congress.

In the Danville case it is to be noted that the Richmond and Danville road had no joint-rate agreement with its connections. Where such agreements exist, the connecting roads should, it seems, as to the joint traffic, be considered as if but a single road, and the charges over one part of the route may properly be taken as a criterion of charges over other parts, or over the whole. In the case of Farrar *vs.* The East Tennessee & Georgia, and the Norfolk & Western Railroad companies (1 Interstate Com. Repts., p. 764), it appeared that the two companies made joint rates on lumber, from Dalton, Georgia, to points on the line of the last-named road in Virginia, though the basis of the division of rates is not given in the opinion in the case.

The local charges on lumber of the E. T., V., & G. Company, over that part of the route from Dalton to Knoxville, a distance of 110 miles, were 7 cts. per cwt., and to Bristol, 241 miles, 11 cts. per cwt., Bristol being the point of connection between the two roads. The joint rates from Dalton to Roanoke, Va., a distance of 391 miles, were 22 cts. per cwt., and to Lynchburg, 445 miles, 22 cts. per cwt. The charges, therefore, were at the rate of 1.27 cts. per ton per mile from Dalton to Knoxville, of .917 cts. per ton mile to Bristol, of 1.12 cts. per ton mile to Roanoke, and of .988 cts. per ton mile to Lynchburg.

Or, treating the Norfolk & Western road independently, the charges from Bristol to Roanoke were at the rate of 1.47 cts. per ton mile, and from Bristol to Lynchburg at the rate of 1.08 cts. per ton mile. The shipments were continuous, there being no break of bulk or rehandling of the lumber at Bristol. Complaint of the charges above referred to, being made to the Interstate Commerce Commission, it was decided that the rates from Dalton to Knoxville and Bristol were not unreasonable. But concerning the joint rates to Roanoke and Lynchburg it was said: " It is a very familiar rule in the transportation of freight by railroads, and has become axiomatic, that while the aggregate charge is continually increasing, the further the freight is carried, yet the rate per ton per mile is constantly growing less all the time. In consequence of the existence of this rule, the aggregate charge continues to be less in proportion every hundred miles after the first, arising out of the character and nature of the service performed, and the cost of the service; and thus it is that staple commodities and merchandise are enabled to bear the charges of transportation, from and to the most distant portions of our country. Examples showing the universality of this rule may be seen in the tariffs of the railroad companies generally in the United States, where their length is sufficient to admit of its application. In the rates charged between Dalton, Knoxville, Johnson City, and Bristol, this rule is observed ; but between Bristol and Roanoke and Lynchburg in this continuous haul it is not. The act to regulate commerce, so far from throwing hampering restrictions or obstacles in the way of the operation of this salutary rule, gives it all the benefit and aid of its sanction and safeguards, by providing that the carrier shall be entitled to recover a reasonable compensation for the service performed upon open published rates against which no competitor can take advantage by allowing shippers secret rebates and drawbacks in order to get the business. . . . The conclusion that we have reached upon the evidence in this case is that the joint rates of 22 cts. charged by the East Tennessee, Virginia, & Georgia, and the Norfolk & Western Railroad companies, upon car-load lots of lumber from Dalton, Georgia, to Roanoake and Lynchburg, Virginia, are each unreasonable, and that 17 cts. per 100 pounds in car-load lots of such lumber from Dalton to Roanoke, and 18 cts. per 100 pounds on car-load lots of such lumber from Dalton to Lynchburg, would be reasonable."

An order was accordingly entered by the commission that the rates should be fixed at those figures.

In the case of Evans *vs.* Oregon Railway & Nav. Co. (1 Interstate Com. Repts., p. 641), where the railroad company was required to reduce its rates on wheat between certain points, the elements entering into the general question of the reasonableness of rates were quite fully considered by the commission. And it was said that "a variety of practical considerations must enter into the making of freight rates by a railroad company, and determine to a great extent, in every instance, the question whether such rates are reasonable or not. Railroad companies can not be required to make freight rates upon mere theories or conjectures. They have to deal with business as they find it."

The practice of "grouping rates," that is, making the same charge for transportation of similar commodities from or to different and sometimes widely separated stations on the same line, has recently engaged the attention of the commission. In the case of the rates on milk coming from the country districts into New York City (to be reported in 2d Interstate Com. Repts.), it appeared that the same charge was imposed for carrying milk 21 miles as for 183 miles, and all intermediate distances on the same road.

This was claimed to confer an undue advantage on the more remote stations and shippers, and to impose an undue disadvantage on those located nearer the city. And it was argued that: "Undue advantage to the one, and undue prejudice to the other, is just as great when the difference is made in the increased amount of the service rendered for the same price, as it is when the difference is made in the increased price charged for the same amount of service." The commission, after referring to numerous instances where the practice of grouping prevails, without, however giving its sanction to the practice, said: "The principle of grouping is not novel. The propriety of its application is properly open to challenge in every case, and every case must be justified upon its own facts and peculiar circumstances." In the case under discussion the application of the grouping principle was sanctioned,—chiefly, it appears, upon two grounds: First, "that the difference in expense to the carrier of the milk traffic" (which was shown to be of an exceptional character) from the different stations " is so trifling that the argument against grouping from this source is not at all controlling, and is in fact of very little weight"; second, that the petitioners "utterly failed to show any way in which they are in fact injured by the grouping of the rates, or by the fact that more distant points have the same rates."

The milk producers near the city, it was said, do not receive any less for their milk because an opportunity is given to those more remote to participate in the industry upon the same terms. " Nor does it appear that there is any glut in the market created by the extension of the identical milk rates, or that there is any difficulty in disposing of the entire . . . product." The commission further remarked that: " In considering a question of this kind, the interests of the public as a whole should be kept in view. It will not do to look solely to the pecuniary advantage of the producers. The great body of consumers are equally entitled to be considered, although their pecuniary interests are individually less, because their number is so much the greater. . . . The system of making a uniform freight rate upon all milk transported upon the same road to a common market, is one of long standing. . . . *It has served the public well. It tends to promote consumption, and to stimulate production."*

The statements contained in the language above italicized, if supported by the facts of the case, as they doubtless are, suggest the real object of the carriers in adopting the grouping principle, and also furnish the justification of the practice. It increases the volume of traffic, and the amount of net earnings to the companies, and it results in the general public benefit.

In the case of Raymond *vs.* R. R. Co. (1 Interstate Com. Repts., p. 627), a railroad company having a branch line, upon which are located towns whose situation fairly entitles them to compete for business with towns on the main line, but of which business they had been deprived by reason of the higher transportation charges imposed upon them, was compelled to readjust its rates in the interest of the towns on the branch line. And this, in spite of the fact that the towns on the main line were shown to be within the competitive influence of an independent road, which necessitated lower charges than might otherwise have been reasonable.

The question of export rates—that is, the allowance to a port of shipment of a rebate from the regular rate, on commodities actually exported—has given considerable trouble, and has not yet been squarely decided. The commission has held that the existence of such a rebate system on exports from Boston, allowed to put that city on a footing with New York in the foreign trade, does not prove that Boston is entitled to the New York rate on commodities not exported. But the question of the legality of the rebate was entirely excluded from the consideration of the case, and any expression of opinion upon it carefully abstained from. The allowance of a lower regular rate to New York than to Boston was sanctioned on the ground of the shorter distance from the west to the former city, the greater volume of traffic, and the greater competition between the traffic routes terminating at New York. (Boston Chamber of Commerce *vs.* R. R. Cos. 1st Interstate Com. Repts., p. 754.)

Preferences between shippers have been firmly repressed by the commission when brought to its attention, and some of the devices for effecting discriminations have been exposed and condemned. An instructive case is that of Rice *vs.* Louisville & Nashville R. R. Co. (1 Interstate Com. Repts., p. 722). That company published a tariff sheet in which rates on kerosene oil shipped in tank cars, and rates on the same product per car-load in barrels, were both given. But the tariff sheet failed to disclose the fact that the company itself furnished no tank cars. Much higher rates were charged for hauling barrelled oil by the car-load in the company's own cars, than were charged for the same estimated weights in tank cars belonging to shippers; and, moreover, the weight in the tank cars was *estimated* merely, and was very frequently less than the actual weight.

The shipper furnishing the tank cars was paid by the

company for their use,—the company having also the privilege of using them for return freight when practicable. George Rice, the complainant in the case, was a large producer and shipper of kerosene and kindred oils, but having no tank cars was obliged to avail himself of the ordinary cars furnished by the company, and shipped his oil, barrelled, in those cars. Rice's principal competitor in business was the Standard Oil Company—long dominant in the oil trade and in the favor of the carriers. This company shipped largely in tank cars (its own property), and appears to have been the principal if not the only shipper using that method of transportation. Rice charged that the difference in rates, between tank shipments and barrel shipments, was made by the railroad company for the express purpose of giving the Standard Oil Company the advantage over all other shippers of kerosene oil. It certainly had that effect, and Rice therefore complained : 1st. That the rates on his barrelled oil were unjust and unreasonably high in themselves; 2d. That the rates per tank constituted a less charge to the Standard Oil Company than to him, for a like and contemporaneous service, under substantially similar circumstances and conditions; and 3d. That the difference in rates per car-load in barrels, and per tank, subjected him to undue and unreasonable prejudice and disadvantage, and gave the Standard Oil Company undue and unreasonable preference and advantage over him.

The defendant, railroad company, insisted that the rate for each mode of transporting oil was "reasonable, in and of itself"; declared that the circumstances and conditions of the two modes of transportation were entirely different; and sought to justify the lesser charge on tank shipments, by the fact: 1st. That the shipper himself furnished the rolling stock—saving the company that expense; 2d. That (as asserted) the risk to the company by such shipments was less than by barrel shipments; and 3d. That (as asserted) the probability of procuring return loads in tank cars was greater. And while admitting the advantage to the shipper of the transportation in tank cars, it was also insisted that that mode of carriage was open on the same terms to all who were willing or able to avail themselves of it.

Hence it was argued that no person was charged a greater or less sum than another for the *same service;* and that no one was subjected to any undue prejudice or disadvantage, or given any undue preference or advantage, where the option was given to all alike to select either the cheaper or the more expensive mode of shipment. In reply to the assertion that the rate for each mode of transporting oil was "reasonable in and of itself," Chairman Cooley explained how the question of the reasonableness of a rate was usually a relative one, involving a comparison with the rates charged on other commodities, and especially on commodities of like kind and value which supply the same demand. Therefore in determining the reasonableness of the charges on barrelled oil, the commission deemed itself "absolutely required to keep in view the disparity which is shown to exist between them, and the rates which the same companies charge upon the same article of merchandise when they receive and transport it in cars furnished by the shippers themselves. That disparity has an inevitable and very important bearing upon the question of reasonableness; *prima facie* it is unjust because it is oppressive, and the defendants are fairly called upon to exhibit good reasons for it." Having shown the fallacy of the idea of a rate being "reasonable in and of itself," the commission proceeded to investigate the reasons advanced by the carrier for giving the lower rates to tank shipments. In answer to the argument that the shipper furnished the tank cars, it was said that it was "properly the business of the railroad company to supply to their customers suitable vehicles of transportation (R. R. Co. *vs.* Pratt, 22 Wall, 123–133) and then to offer their use to everybody impartially." And this was declared to be "a very forcible reason why the carrier should see to it that its patrons, who are forced to make use of such facilities as it provides for them, shall not find its own want of rolling stock made a ground of discrimination against them." And it was held that "the fact that one consignor furnishes a car for hire to the railroad company for the transportation of his oil, is no ground whatever for a discrimination in rates in his favor, as against another consignor who must ship in the cars the carrier supplies." In respect to the second and third reasons assigned for favoring tank shipments, namely, the lesser risk and the greater probability of return loads, the commission was of opinion that the evidence did not sustain either claim. Reference was made to the custom of making the rate on tank cars regardless of weight or quantity, as an additional proof of discrimination; especially when the public was led to suppose that when the contents of the car exceeded a certain quantity or weight an extra charge was made, when in fact this was never done. Accordingly an order was entered requiring the companies to make the same car-load rate *per hundred* on kerosene carried in tank cars, as on the same product transported in barrels—including in the latter case the weight of barrels as well as of their contents.

In the case of Providence Coal Co. *vs.* P. & W. R. R. Co. (1 Interstate Com. Repts., 363), the commission decided against a rebate or discount in favor of a large shipper, though the same discount was offered by the railroad company to all dealers who would furnish the same quantity of freight.

"A distinction in rates," says Chairman Cooley, "as between car-loads and smaller quantities, is readily understood and appreciated. . . . But when a question of rebates or discounts is under consideration, it might be misleading to consider them in the light of the principles which merchants act upon in the case of wholesale and retail transactions. There is a very manifest difficulty in applying those principles to the conveniences which common carriers furnish to the public, a difficulty which springs from the nature of the duty which such carriers owe to the public. That duty is one of entire impartiality of service. . . . The carrier cannot regard its own interest exclusively. If it could it might, by methods easily available, drive all small dealers off its line, and centre the whole trade in a few hands. The state of things which would result might be altogether for its interest and convenience . . . but the wrong would be flagrant."

The case of Pyle *vs.* R. R. Co. (1 Interstate Com. Repts., p. 767) involved a complaint of unjust discrimination against "*pearline,*" in favor of common soap, in the classification of the Southern Railway & Steamship Association. Pearline was placed in fourth class, and the rate per hundred pounds from New York to Atlanta was seventy-nine cents, while common soap was placed in sixth class, where the rate was forty-nine cents per hundred ; and to Atlanta there was a special rate on common soap of thirty-three cents per hundred. The transportation was from New York to Norfolk by water, and thence to Atlanta by rail, in part over the road complained of. It appeared that common soap and pearline were put up and transported in packages of similar size, shape, and weight, and that there was no practical difference in the cost of service in transporting either article. It also appeared that common soap and pearline are used for the same general purposes, and are, therefore, competitive in commerce; and in all the classifications except that of the S. R. & S. S. Association they are placed in the same class.

The railroad company sought to justify the difference in classification on the ground that the market value of pearline was about double that of common soap, and that (as asserted) the risk of loss or injury in transportation is much greater in case of the former than the latter. The commission held that these reasons justified a difference in the classification, but not so great as that which had been established; and it was ordered that "while common soap is in its sixth class, pearline must be placed in its fifth class," which would impose a rate of sixty cents per hundred on the latter article from New York to Atlanta. The commission, in coming to its conclusions, relied largely upon the difference in value of the commodities as justifying a difference in classification, and also laid great weight upon the alleged difference in risk. And a greater difference in the classification was allowed, by reason of the transportation being partly by water, than would have been had it been "all rail," it being supposed that the relative risk of damage was greater by water than by rail. The competitive character of the two articles, on the other hand, had weight with the commission to make the difference allowed less than might have been justified in the absence of that consideration. It would seem probable that undue weight was given in this case to the argument of relative risk in the carriage of the two commodities, as the evidence failed to show that any damage in transportation had ever occurred, or would be likely to occur, to pearline, beyond what common soap might also sustain.

The difference in the value of the article undoubtedly affords a sound basis for difference in classification.

In the case of Reynolds *vs.* R. R. Co. (vol. 1 Interstate Com. Repts., p. 685), it appeared that the company had placed railroad ties in fifth class, and lumber and other coarse products of the forest in sixth class, the rate on the fifth being considerably higher than on the sixth class of traffic.

But besides the discrimination thus made in the regular tariff, against cross-ties as compared with lumber, the latter was in practice constantly given a special rate, about one half that on ties. Complaint of this discrimination against traffic in cross-ties being made to the commission, that tribunal found, as a matter of fact, that there was no difference in cost of service, in risk, or in the value of the commodity to justify classifying cross-ties higher than lumber; and it further found that there was no competition with other roads in the lumber traffic to justify the special low rate charged on lumber as compared with the rate on ties. The sole motive of the discrimination was plainly to prevent the ties going off the line of the road, and to enable the company to purchase them at its own figures. The commission in terms of very just censure against the injustice of this discrimination forbade its further continuance,—concluding the opinion in the case as follows: " Rates established by a common carrier under the influence of a desire to keep upon its line a material for which the road itself has use, or to keep the price thereof low for its own advantage, cannot be justified either in morals or in law. Every party who produces such a material is entitled to sell it when he wishes in the best available market, and the common carrier has no right to prevent his doing so by disproportionate or unreasonable rates. This the defendants in the present case have been attempting to do."

The most interesting and important question involving the classification of freights yet presented to the commission has not been decided, the complaints involving it having been withdrawn. It arose in the complaints preferred by the producers and shippers of dressed meat, of excessive charges imposed on the transportation of their product as compared with the rates for the transportation of live stock. Of course the expense and risk to the carriers of handling the dressed-meat traffic is considerably greater than that incident to the live-stock business. It seems to be generally conceded, however, that the difference in charge was greater than could be justified by the mere difference in cost and risk, and on the general ground of charging according to "what the traffic will bear," a further difference in rates may certainly be justified.

But there seems to be a specific and important public reason why the transportation charges on dressed meat should considerably exceed those on live stock; and this is that the live-stock business, and the traffic in beef cattle, etc., between the butchers of the cities and the small graziers throughout the country, may not be destroyed, as it probably would be under any thing like equal rates.

This subject has already been adverted to. Dressed meat and live stock are competitive commodities in commerce, and the relative rates on each should be so adjusted and maintained as to promote and not destroy the competition. This principle was recognized in the case (heretofore commented on) involving the relative rates on pearline and soap. In that instance the rates on the two commodities were, in the interest of competition, more nearly approximated to each other. But the same principle requires the maintenance of a proper disparity in rates where necessary to preserve the competition of products. It may be safely anticipated that the commission, if called on to decide this question—involving as it does results of such vital importance,—will be guided by those considerations which point to the security and protection of the public as its first and highest duty.

Senator Cullom, to whose untiring zeal and conservative temperament the enactment of the Interstate Commerce Law in its present shape was largely due, in a recent speech in the Senate reviewed the results of the first year's operation of the act. From this it appears that one of the immediate effects of the law was the abandonment of all pools upon interstate traffic. The associations through which pooling was carried on have, however, been reorganized, and continued to carry out the other objects for which they were formed, such as the making of regulations for the interchange of traffic, the arrangement of classifications, the making of joint rates, and numerous other matters of detail. It is generally believed that the division of business and the diversion of freights, which were among the most objectionable features of the pooling system, have ceased; but the existing traffic associations still manage to control the rates on certain classes of important traffic as effectively and as arbitrarily as they did in the palmiest days of the old pooling system. Another noticeable effect of the act was the immediate termination of a vast number of special freight contracts and agreements, under which rebates and drawbacks had been paid to favored shippers. Greater uniformity of classification has also resulted. The provisions requiring publication of rates, and forbidding departure from the same as published, in connection with the long- and short-haul rule, have rendered the rate wars which have occurred since the passage of the act much more disastrous in their effect upon the revenues of the carriers than those which previously took place. Formerly such wars could be carried on, in respect to long-distance traffic between competitive points, without any reduction whatever at local stations on either road engaged in the cutting of rates.

Those which have since been indulged in, except the one waged by the trans-continental lines and the Canadian Pacific, have resulted in reductions at intermediate stations, and have affected very seriously the revenues of the competing roads from their own local traffic. In a number of cases (some of which have been reviewed) where questions of the reasonableness of rates or of discriminations have been brought before the commission, it has ordered a reduction of the rates, or the abandonment of the discriminative practice. And the decisions in these cases have had an influence far beyond the questions and parties immediately involved. They have established principles, have been accepted as precedents, and have affected rates throughout the country. The tendency of railroad rates in general, since the passage of the law, has been downward, and though it cannot be claimed that this has been always or entirely due to the Interstate Commerce Act, that has undoubtedly been potential in securing a reduction of rates in many instances. One class of reductions must be directly attributed to the operation of the law. These are where under the former practice more was charged for a shorter than a longer distance over the same line in the same direction, the shorter being included within the longer distance. When the law took effect a very large majority of the carriers of the country entirely revolutionized their practice in this respect, and framed their tariffs in accordance with the prohibition against a greater charge for the shorter than for the longer haul. In doing this the local rates were generally reduced, without the through rates being raised. As illustrative of this result, which has occurred in many sections of the Union, it may be stated that rates on grain from western Illinois to the Atlantic seaboard are now, for the first time, no higher than the rates from St. Louis. The same is true of rates from western Missouri and Iowa, as compared with the rates from Kansas City and Omaha respectively. And in general it appears that throughout the vast territory of the northern Mississippi valley, this feature of the law has operated to the manifest advantage of shippers of produce from the smaller towns and stations. Nearly all of the leading roads of the eastern, middle, and central States are said to be complying strictly with the statute.

But in large sections of country where competition with water routes more or less directly prevails,—and especially in the southern States,—the railroad companies have assumed to consider their circumstances and conditions as bringing them within the exceptions to the general rule, and are, by no means, universally complying with it.

Such are some of the results of the Interstate Commerce Law, as viewed from the standpoint of a friendly critic. On the other hand, it is to be said that the law has been ineffectual to prevent wars of rates, a number of which, of unusual violence, have occurred since it took effect.

This is not surprising, as the prohibition of pooling deprived the railroads of the only reasonably effective means yet devised, of preventing this disastrous species of excessive competition. Before the era of pooling, the certainty of financial disaster from rate wars did not prevent their constant occurrence; and the check which some supposed would be placed upon them by the operation of the long- and short-haul rule has evidently not been successful. While non-competitive points may not have been placed at the same disadvantage as heretofore during this state of things, yet it is not improbable that very pernicious discriminations have been practised under some covert form. And this suspicion is largely confirmed by the recent disclosure of the system of underbilling, which since the passage of the act has prevailed more extensively than ever before. It is plain, too, that the taking of traffic at less than reasonable figures may result in injury to other companies than those which participate in the cut of rates. The companies which are conservative enough to hold aloof from the strife may lose more or less business which, under the usual and normal adjustment of traffic charges, they would receive. This loss, if continued, must result in detriment not only to the carriers, but thereby to the local communities which they serve. These considerations, as well as the general desirability of steadiness in rates, make it to the interest of the public as well as the carriers that wars of rates should cease. The difficulty of checking them is greatly increased by the fact that the commission has no authority (as it has decided) to protect a conservative company against the cut-throat competition of a rival. It is not improbable, however, that the vital necessity for concert of action between competing lines will suggest some device which, while not falling within the prohibition of the law against pooling, will in a measure accomplish the results the pooling system was intended to secure, in maintaining traffic charges and preventing ruinous strife. During the present year (1889) much attention has been attracted by the efforts of some of the leading western roads to perfect an association with the avowed purpose of "enforcement of the Interstate Commerce Law, and the arbitration of all differences between companies." An important feature of the scheme is the provision intended to place the responsibility for the maintenance of traffic charges directly upon the principal officers of the companies, and to minimize the powers of subordinates in this respect. Some of the leading financiers of the country participated in the conferences, which resulted in the formation of the "Interstate Commerce Railway Association." A member of the Federal Railroad Commission was called to the position of executive head of the association, and resigned his public office to accept it. Considerable faith was felt in the stability of this organization, and in its effectiveness for the prevention of hostile action between the parties to it. Unfortunately the first severe test to which it has been put has resulted in the withdrawal of one of the leading companies from the association, and the resumption by it of an independent policy; an act which forcibly illustrates the truth of a prominent traffic manager's remark that "additional pledges as distinguished from additional means of enforcement seem likely to be of very little use, even though they be executed with the greatest solemnity." The permanence and increasing usefulness of the association is, however, by no means despaired of by its friends on account of this defection, and for the present at least, peaceful conditions appear to prevail among its members.

But even where no actual warfare exists between competitive companies, and traffic charges are so adjusted as to comply with the provisions of the law, and at the same time produce adequate revenues *to the stronger lines*, the situation of the *weaker lines* is both injuriously and unjustly affected by the long- and short-haul rule. Its tendency is beneficial to the former, but detrimental to the latter, and is apt in the long run to be detrimental to the local patrons of the latter also. Its operation in many cases certainly looks like diminishing the revenues of the weak lines without benefiting their patrons; and should a case be presented where the law is proven to have this effect, its application to such a case could hardly be judicially allowed. That the tendency towards the unification and consolidation of different and competitive lines has been decidedly increased by the anti-pooling and the long- and short-haul sections of the Interstate

Commerce Law can hardly be doubted. It has been mentioned that many of the railroad companies in the territory south of the Potomac and Ohio and east of the Mississippi have assumed to operate under the exception to the fourth section of the act, and to charge in many cases a greater amount in the aggregate for a shorter than for a longer distance over the same line in the same direction, the shorter being included within the longer distance. Recently the Commission determined upon a general revision of railroad rates in the territory named, with the view of bringing them more nearly within the requirements of the general rule as to long and short hauls. Such action under the conditions of traffic and of competition in the South seemed to threaten no little peril to the finances of various lines and systems operating independently within that territory.

Pooling was forbidden by the federal law, but the far more radical and effective method of destroying competition, by consolidation of the different companies, or by the acquisition in the same hands of controlling interests in each, was necessarily left to the legislation of the States. Among the most important of the southern railway systems is the Richmond & Danville, which ramifies through the Carolinas, Georgia, and Alabama, and reaches the North by an all-rail route via Washington city, or by rail and water via West Point, Virginia.

Among its principal competitors were the Central Railroad of Georgia (operating a network of roads in that and other States, and a steamship line via Savannah to the North), and the East Tennessee, Virginia, & Georgia Railroad, having its principal northern outlet over the Norfolk & Western. The Richmond & Danville acquired interests in the E. Tenn., Va., & Georgia, early in the year 1887; but soon after the determination of the Interstate Commerce Commission to revise the railroad rates of the South was made public, the financial world was startled by the announcement that the two last-named railway systems, and also the Georgia Central, embracing in the aggregate some 7,000 miles of road, had, through the instrumentality of the Richmond & West Point Terminal Company, been all brought under a common control and management.[1] The acquisition of still other properties under the same management is suggested, and will probably be ultimately accomplished. This condition of things may be almost directly attributed to the Interstate Commerce Law. By prohibiting pooling, that measure invited consolidation. It destroyed a confederacy, and an empire rises from the ruins. In an interview with Mr. John H. Inman, president of the Richmond Terminal Company, as published in the *Atlanta Constitution* of November 11, 1888, he is reported as having said, concerning the effect of this railway combination on the commercial and industrial interests of the South: " We propose to make Savannah by far the most

---

[1] Certain legal obstacles have, however, since arisen in the way of this combination.

important of all southern seaports. To do this, it will, of course, be necessary to take away a great part of the business which now goes to Norfolk. . . . Instead of making Norfolk our coast-distributing point, we shall turn our commerce southward, and deliver it at Brunswick and Savannah, each of which ports will be vastly benefited."

This language suggests one of the dangerous results that may follow upon the concentration in a few hands of such power over the commerce of a vast territory. If the traffic of the region controlled by the Terminal Company, or of any part of it, has heretofore, by an inequitable adjustment of traffic charges, been diverted from its natural channels to Norfolk; and if under a fair and natural arrangement of charges and facilities it would seek its tide-water outlet at Savannah or Brunswick, then it is proper that Norfolk should to that extent be the loser and the more southern ports the gainers. But, if Mr. Inman is correctly reported, the railway management does not propose to let the traffic originating on the lines of his system (" our commerce," he calls it) seek its own outlet. On the contrary, he declares that: " Instead of making Norfolk our coast-distributing point, we shall turn our commerce southward." If this diversion of traffic is to be accomplished by making rates and connections and offering facilities in one direction, which are refused in another, merely for the purpose of building up one port and injuring its rival, or of forcing traffic over one route which naturally would pass over another, it is apt to meet with difficulties in the provisions of the Interstate Commerce Law. Perhaps Mr. Inman merely meant that under the changed condition of things a large amount of the business now done through Norfolk would naturally go to Savannah and Brunswick; and this may be true. It is not likely that any improper means will be attempted to deprive Norfolk of its legitimate business, or if attempted that it will be permitted. Upon the whole, there is nothing in this combination of railway interests to excite public apprehension. Compliance with the law and with the requirements of the commission is facilitated, many elements of injustice to shippers and of discord between the carriers are eliminated, and the general public, as well as the railroad companies, are unquestionably benefited by the result.

The modern device of the "trust," as a means of unifying industrial interests and eliminating competition, has not yet been applied in the field of railroad transportation. An approach to it is exhibited in the operation of the Richmond Terminal Company above referred to, where the capacity of that corporation for the acquisition and ownership of the stock of other companies has been largely utilized. This, however, presents a different case from a "railway trust," which, by analogy to other industrial combinations to which that name has been given, would be effected by a surrender of the stock (and with it the controlling power) of each separate company into the hands of trustees, in exchange for "trust certificates," bearing such ratio in amount to the par value of the shares in the several companies, as might be agreed on in the instrument creating the trust. The several properties thus fall under the management of a single board, namely the trustees, who, holding the stock, may name the directory and direct the policy of each company. The joint aggregate amount of net earnings is distributed among the holders of trust certificates,—the stockholders in the respective companies as such having in the distribution of profits disappeared from consideration.

The scheme of trust here briefly outlined, would probably require for its successful operation the concurrence of the entire stockholding interest of each company embraced in it; and herein it seems likely will be found the chief difficulty in perfecting such a scheme. Should it ever be perfected, a far more stringent public supervision and control of the railroad transportation of the country, will inevitably be demanded.

CHAPTER IX.

EXPRESS TRAFFIC.

The Relations of Express to Railroad Carriers one of Contract Merely—Effect of Wars of Express Rates on Railway Charges and Earnings—The Express Company the Means of Warfare between Rival Railroads—The Case of the Express Companies before Congress and the Commission.

THE express business, which now embraces a large and increasing amount of traffic which was formerly carried on by the railroads as freight business, has not generally been made the subject of public regulation. There can scarcely be any doubt, however, of the right of public regulation of these agencies of commerce; for this right is not based exclusively upon the corporate character of the agency or the grant to it of the power of eminent domain, but exists wherever capital or property " is used in a manner to make it of public consequence and affect the community at large." (Munn *vs.* Illinois, *supra.*)

The legal status of the express companies is undoubtedly that of common carriers, and such they have frequently been held to be, although in connection with the carrying business they may perform other services. (Redfield on Railways, vol. ii., pp. 4, 24.)

There are ten or twelve principal express carriers operating in the United States, and several of them—enjoying perhaps the most extensive and widely ramifying business of any—are not incorporated companies; but though interests in them are evidenced by transferable shares of stock, the shareholders are nevertheless liable as partners among themselves and to the public.

Of course the express companies have to avail themselves largely of railroad facilities. Usually they do not own the cars on which their freight is carried; but they contract with the railroad companies for necessary facilities on their trains, either by renting so much car space, or by paying a certain price for estimated or actual weight of freight, or (which is the most usual method), by an agreement for division of the gross earnings received by the express company, for its entire service in respect to the article transported. "The reason is obvious why special contracts in reference to this kind of business are necessary. The transportation required is of a kind which must, if possible, be had for the most part on passenger trains. It requires not only speed, but reasonable certainty as to the quantity that will be carried at any one time. As the things carried are to be kept in the personal custody of the messenger or other employé of the express company, it is important that a certain amount of car space should be specifically set apart for the business, and that this should, as far as practicable, be put in the exclusive possession of the expressman in charge."

The agreement between the railroad and the express

company therefore, always includes the carriage of the express messenger, in personal custody of the freight. The express companies are recognized as district carriers from the railroad companies, and the latter are frequently exempted by statutory provisions from liability as carriers to the owners of express freight consigned by way of an independent express company which uses their lines.

Some railroad companies, however, undertake to do their own express business, without the aid or intervention of a different agency; and in some cases there are associations of connecting railroad companies for the purpose of carrying express traffic in a manner quite analogous to that adopted in the Dispatch Freight lines.

The usual facilities are furnished for the business, similar to those furnished by the express companies, and the carriage is usually on passenger trains, with a special agent in personal charge of the freight.

So that a shipper desiring to forward by express, on railroad lines which do their own express business, may generally have, upon paying the proper additional freight charges, substantially the same facilities as those afforded by the independent express companies.

It is evident, though, from what has been said, that very different arrangements and accommodations are necessary for handling the express traffic, from those which are used in handling the ordinary freight; rendering almost indispensable a separate department for the management of the express business, where the latter is of any considerable magnitude. And it has been found difficult by some railroad companies to render proper express facilities to the public and at the same time make that branch of their service remunerative to themselves. Accordingly they have surrendered the express business over their lines to some one of the regular express companies under contract as above described.

Under these contracts the railroad company becomes the carrier of a carrier, and the rights and obligations of the parties arise out of the contract only, the railroad companies being under no legal obligation in the absence of statutory requirements, to furnish to express carriers the special facilities which these contracts usually provide.

The claim has been made by express companies, that, independent of any contract with railroad companies, they are entitled to have from the latter all facilities and accommodations for carrying express freight over railroad lines, which are usually accorded by the contracts between express and railroad companies.

In the "Express Cases" (117 U. S., p. 1), one of the suits was that of the Southern Express Co. as plaintiff, against the St. L., I. M., & S. R. R. Co., as defendant. Among other things the plaintiff prayed: "That the said defendant may be decreed by this court to transport at all times the express matter, safes, and messengers of the said Southern Express Co., by the same trains and with the same accommodations thereon, and in its depots and stations, as it may transport its own express matter, or as it may accord to itself."

In answer it was said that: "Defendant claims the right to carry and transport what is called express matter in the spaces in its cars selected by itself, and under the supervision, care, and control of its own employés, and has refused, and does refuse to complainant, the right to have allotted to itself any particular space in defendant's express cars, for its exclusive use, or to permit its messengers to ride in the express cars, and to take charge of complainant's express freight."

The railroad company, however, having undertaken to do the express business over its line on its own account, avowed its willingness to take and carry any express matter or freight that the express company, as any ordinary shipper, might offer to it.

The United States Circuit Court in Kansas, where the original suit was instituted, held and decreed, among other things (Justice Miller of the United States Supreme Court sitting and concurring): "That it is the duty of the defendant to carry the express matter of the plaintiff's company, and the messengers or agents in charge thereof, at a just and reasonable rate of compensation; and that such compensation is to be found and established as a unit, and is to include as well the transportation of such messengers or agents, as of the express matter in their custody and under their control."

And the court further undertook to prescribe, by its

decree, the terms, the manner, and the extent to which the railroad companies should give facilities to the express companies.

But when the case came on appeal before the Supreme Court of the United States, the decree of the Circuit Court was reversed, and it was held that, in the absence of legislation for the purpose, the courts cannot compel railroad companies to enter into such arrangements with express carriers. Chief-Justice Waite delivered the opinion of the court (from which, however, Justices Miller and Field dissented), in the course of which it was said: "So long as the public are served to their reasonable satisfaction, it is a matter of no importance who serves them. The railroad company performs its whole duty to the public at large, and to each individual, when it affords the public all reasonable express accommodations. If this is done, the railroad company owes no duty to the public, as to the particular agencies it shall select for that purpose. The public require the carriage, but the company may choose its own appropriate means of carriage, always provided they are such as to insure reasonable promptness and security." And it was further said that: "The regulation of matters of this kind is legislative in its character, not judicial. To what extent it must come, if it comes at all, from Congress, and to what extent it may come from the States, are questions we do not now undertake to decide; but that it must come, when it does come, from some source of legislative power, we do not doubt. The legislature may impose a duty, and when imposed it will if necessary be enforced by the courts, but unless a duty has been created, either by usage or by contract or by statute, the courts cannot be called on to give it effect." Under this decision, the railroad companies, in the absence of legislation imposing additional duties, may do their own express business, or may employ for the purpose the agency of one or more of the independent express companies.

Each railroad company, as a general rule, only admits one express company to the use of its express facilities, so that on any particular line of road, the express company has the same monopoly and control of its traffic, as the railroad company has of its ordinary freight traffic. Nor is there any peculiarity in the express traffic, or any distinction between it and many kinds of common freight, except in the method of transportation.

In other words, there are many articles usually carried as common freight, which the shipper may, if special speed and care are desirable, or if the express companies offer better terms, send by express. Usually the contracts between the railroads and express companies provide that the latter shall not carry such articles as may conveniently be taken as ordinary freight, except at rates considerably higher than first class railroad freight rates. This provision is of course intended to prevent the express company from unduly encroaching on the classes of traffic which the railroad companies can conveniently and profitably handle themselves. And it is easy to see that but for this limitation on its charges, the express company might easily, by sufficiently reducing its rates, take from the railroad a very large proportion of its most valuable and hence most profitable traffic. Where different express companies operate over two or more lines of railroad which at certain points are competitive, it is evident that there may be competition for the express business at the same points; and it is probable that the contract stipulation above referred to, fixing the express rates at figures considerably higher than those on the same articles carried as common freight, is the principal safeguard against wars of express rates, similar to such as have frequently prevailed between railroad companies. This in part accounts for the fact that complaints of discrimination between places and persons have been much less common against express than against railroad companies.

Abuses of this sort do, however, exist, and while operating *pro tanto* the same kind of public injury as arises from railroad freight discriminations, they may also very seriously impair the revenues of some of the railway lines over which the express carriers operate. In fact the express company may be made the instrument of warfare by one railroad company against another, its competitor. For example, two cities, between which there is a heavy express traffic, are connected by two independent lines of railroad, over each of which a different express company operates. For some reason, one of these lines is better adapted for the service than the other, and consequently the bulk of the express business passes over it. The other railroad company, seeing this, absolves its express company from the stipulation in regard to rates, and leaves it free to make such reductions as will take the express freight from the rival line, and perhaps a considerable amount of the high-class railroad freight also.

The latter company, both to retain its own traffic, and to enable the express company with which it coöperates to do the same, is compelled by its adversaries' action also to dispense with the provision against a reduction of express charges. The inevitable result is the transfer of the most lucrative portion of the freight traffic into the hands of the express companies, causing a serious drain on the railway revenues; while in the operation of the express business there are sure to follow those secret rebates, unfair personal discriminations, and relatively unjust charges to non-competitive points, which have aroused so much public odium against the railroad transportation system. That these conditions of excessive competition have not more frequently arisen in the express transportation system is also largely due to the fact that the number of competitors is very small compared with the number of competitive railroad lines, and to the further fact that the express companies, either by express or tacit understanding, have to a large extent parcelled out the territory of the country among themselves, so that points of hostile contact between them are comparatively few.

From the foregoing explanation of the relations between the railroad and the express companies, it is easy to see how easily regulative legislation which embraces the former companies alone, may be evaded by a simple modification of existing arrangements between these co-operative carriers. Hence it would seem to be plain that any legislation for the regulation of transportation by railroad should embrace the independent express companies, so far as they do business over railroad lines.

It is somewhat singular that in all the discussions in Congress on the subject of railway regulation, which preceded the passage of the act for that purpose, and in the many volumes of testimony and reports concerning it, there is little or nothing bearing on the relations of the express to the common freight traffic, and the propriety of including the former in the terms of statutory regulation.

Very soon after the organization of the Interstate Commerce Commission, the question was presented whether the express companies of the country had been placed by the act of Congress under its jurisdiction. Counsel for the express companies urged many arguments against the jurisdiction of the commission over that class of carriers; some of a general character, applicable to any regulative legislation; but mostly directed to the phraseology and constitutionality of certain sections of the Interstate Commerce Act. It was suggested rather than asserted, that express companies so far as they use railway facilities, are not common carriers in the usual acceptation of the term, but stand in the relation rather of shippers by rail.

It was pointed out, too, that these companies render to their patrons many other services besides that of carrying or forwarding—such as collecting money, indorsing and protesting negotiable paper, attending to the recordation of deeds, giving bonds to clear goods at custom-houses, and other matters not directly connected with transportation.

Great stress was laid upon the fact that horse- and wagon-service for the collection and delivery of packages, and for making connection between different railway stations in the cities, constitutes a very large and essential element of the express business. Attention was called to the very general use of steamboat and stage-coach lines by the express companies, as distinguishing them from carriers wholly by railroad. The fact that many of these companies are unincorporated, and that none of them had ever been granted or had exercised the public right of eminent domain, was alluded to in the arguments. It was somewhat confidently asserted that the public evils which gave rise to popular complaints against the railroad transportation system had no place in the express business; and in support of this assertion the debates in Congress, the reports of committees, and the testimony taken by them were referred to as containing not a syllable of complaint against the express companies. The frequent allusion to express companies by name, in other acts of Congress, was contrasted with the entire absence of any mention of them in the Interstate Commerce Act, as strongly indicating the absence of any legislative intent to include them in the latter. It was declared that a strict enforcement against the express companies of the requirements of the act in regard to publication and posting of rates would entail an expense on them of many millions of dollars, and the printing of a volume of matter almost beyond conception.

Many of the requirements and prohibitions of the act, it was said, related to matters wholly foreign to the express business, and it was contended that all its provisions should be strictly construed, because of the penalties imposed for their violation.

If so construed, in the light of all the circumstances surrounding the origin and enactment of the law, and of the well-known public evils it was designed to remedy, it was confidently maintained that the express companies could not be included within its provisions, or brought under the jurisdiction of the commission. The immediate question which gave rise to the consideration of the status of the express companies under the Interstate Commerce Act was that of their objection to publish their rates and file schedules thereof with the commission. Some of the companies acknowledged the obligation and filed their schedules, but others, for reasons advanced by them, and just referred to, denied the obligation. Many of these reasons the commission considered insufficient,

The legal status of express companies as common carriers was assumed without discussion, and it was said that " there is no reason apparent, in the case of express companies, why the obligations and restrictions of the act should not be held effective upon their business, so far as it is applicable thereto, arising from the mere fact that other business is also done by them, to which those provisions are inapplicable, or that sometimes a further service than that of transportation is performed in respect to the articles carried."

Again : " Their exclusion from the operation of the statute, upon the ground that in cities and large towns it is customary for express companies to collect and deliver freight, would seem to be too refined a construction to be placed upon the law. Some railroads do the same thing, and it is much more common in England than here."

The extravagant statements as to the cost of publishing express rates, and the enormous bulk of the publication, was met by the commission by a reference to the fact that several of the express companies had already filed their schedules with the commission, " and although the tariffs so filed are made up on different plans, yet they are each intelligible, and are sufficient to negative the idea that the thing proposed by Congress is not possible of accomplishment by this class of carriers." And, " in fact, it seems necessary that agents of express companies should be instructed explicitly as to charges to be made by them, and if they can be intelligently notified by instructions from the general offices, it would seem quite possible to inform the public also." Again it was said: "Looking at the sections of the act in detail, so far as they declare principles or announce requirements, and they will be seen to be quite generally applicable as well to the business of express companies as to that of railroad companies." And "while this statute contains certain provisions for penalties, . . . nevertheless, the statute as a whole should be regarded as highly remedial in its provisions," and hence should be construed fairly and liberally, and not with that strictness applicable to a penal enactment."

"It would seem, therefore," to quote further from the opinion of the commission, "that the bringing of the express companies within the salutary provisions of the act to regulate commerce is practicable and on some accounts desirable. The question remains whether or not this has been accomplished by the statute as it stands.

"In respect to some of the express companies, there can be little if any doubt that they are fully subject to the provisions of the law. When a railroad company itself conducts the parcel traffic on its line by its ordinary transportation staff, or through an independent bureau organized for the purpose, or by means of a combination with other railroad companies, in a joint arrangement for the transaction of this so-called express business, it will not be seriously questioned, but that this branch of the traffic is subject to the act to regulate commerce as fully as the ordinary freight traffic. But the case of the independently organized express companies must be more carefully considered."

And in respect to them it was said that: "A careful examination of the history and the language of the act to regulate commerce has brought the commission to the conclusion that the independent express companies are not included among the common carriers declared to be subject to its provisions as they now stand. The fact that a part of the express business of the country is, as above shown, within the act, while another and a much larger part of the same business is not so described as to be embraced in the same statute, clearly points out the necessity of further legislative action. Either the entire express business should be left wholly on one side, or it should all be included."

The commission, in its first annual report, argues even more strongly the necessity of further action of Congress, for the purpose of either expressly including the independent express companies in the terms of the law, or else of exempting from its operation the express business as carried on by the railroad companies themselves.

Although it is not in terms advised that Congress should adopt either one of these suggestions in preference to the other, yet the conclusion seems almost irresistible, from the argument of the commission, that the independent express companies should be brought under the operation of the act. For it is declared in the report that: "The railroad companies, which see fit to do their own express business, ought not, either as respects principles or methods, to be subjected in the management of such business to any different control or regulation from that which the independent express companies of the country are required to obey. If the latter are not within the contemplation of the act to regulate commerce, all express business, by whomsoever carried on, should be excluded."

While to show how subversive of the intent and the benefits of the act the adoption of the latter alternative would be, it is also said, "that no clear line of distinction exists between the express business and some branches of what is exclusively railroad service; and the express business may easily be enlarged at the expense of the other. Those roads which now do their own express business, through a nominal corporation, might hand over to this shadow of their corporate existence the dressed-meat or live-stock business, or the fruit transportation, or any other business in respect to which speed was specially important; and they might continue this process of pairing off their proper functions as carriers, until they should be little more than the owners of lines of road over which other organizations should be the carriers of freight, and on terms by themselves arbitrarily determined." It is also remarked by the commission that: "The complaint of excessive charges upon express traffic has been common, and that of greater charges on shorter hauls has been sometimes heard, and if it shall be held that express companies are not controlled by the rules of fairness and equality which the act prescribes, it is easy to see that the mischief against which the act is aimed may reappear and be enacted with impunity." The report also calls the attention of Congress to the propriety of embracing in the act certain other carriers who, though they conduct their transportation over railroad lines, are so far distinct from the railroad companies proper, as probably not to be included in the existing law. For, as very justly observed: "The act has not changed the nature or the grasping disposition of individuals; it has only interposed certain restraints which, it is reasonable to assume, will be evaded if the opportunity shall be presented."

At the last session of Congress bills were introduced looking to the inclusion of express companies, sleeping-car companies, and other ancillary carriers within the terms of the Interstate Commerce Law. But, after consideration, the committee to whom they were referred deemed it best "to perfect the system of regulation now on the statute-book, rather than attempt to enlarge it."

The express companies have therefore, for the present at least, been left free to conduct their interstate-traffic operations according to their own views of expediency and justice, untrammelled by public intervention.

In conclusion it may be remarked that representatives of the railway interests not infrequently assert that the public demand for railway regulation is the work of aspiring politicians in search of a popular issue. No doubt demagogues have availed themselves of public feeling on the subject to promote selfish ends, and have magnified evils and aggravated antagonisms.

But the mere fact of its popularity indicates a substantial basis for the general sentiment on the question; and the light that has been thrown upon it by impartial investigations—with the advantage in presentation always on the side of the railways,—leaves no doubt that there are real and great evils which have aroused public feeling and call for public intervention.

The principal obstacles in the way of proper legislation upon this subject are lack of information, and lack of confidence (or sometimes over-confidence) in the class of men who should be best able to impart it—that is, the railway officials. To investigate the sources of information upon this complex problem, to analyze conflicting testimony, and weigh the merits of opposing arguments, requires an amount of labor and of concentrated thought which in the course of an ordinary legislative session cannot easily be bestowed. The requisite knowledge must be obtained from without, and naturally and properly the railway interest will have its representatives on hand at every session ready from their standpoint to enlighten the legislative mind. Undiscriminating condemnation of this class of persons would be grossly unjust to many fair-minded men who are to be found among them, and who would scorn active participation in the duplicity of associates with whom they are perhaps involuntarily thrown. But it is not to be denied that the character, conduct, and methods of others are such as to raise in the minds of many, who would not wittingly do injustice, the most profound distrust of the entire class. This leads some to reject as mere plausible falsehoods, arguments and suggestions which should have the most careful consideration, and it tends to produce, and has frequently produced, legislation of an extreme and unwarrantable character. On the other hand, in all legislative bodies will be found many members who are very receptive of the class of arguments which lead to the principle of entire non-interference, and to the defeat of all attempts at public regulation.

In extenuation of the course too frequently pursued by railway representatives to influence or defeat legislative action, should be mentioned a sentiment, not easy of satisfactory explanation, perhaps, but deeply rooted in many minds, which seems to regard the railway corporation as the natural enemy and oppressor of the masses of the people, to be despoiled and warred upon whenever occasion offers. This sentiment is responsible for the extravagant and questionable—not to say unconscionable —verdicts frequently rendered by juries against railroad companies, and for the extreme legislation which has sometimes been enacted against them.

Public animosity towards the railways, and the questionable defensive methods of the latter, act and react upon each other, and both are aggravated. A sincere effort to arrive at truth and justice on the one hand, and a frank disclosure and explanation of the elements of the situation on the other, can alone produce permanent and satisfactory results.

THE END.

The Science of the Hand.

"To him the hand is more than a grammar; even a full-flavored "Ollendorf" would not contain as much language as is to be found within the limits of a palm. Past, present, and future are not only visible to his unerring eye, but the whole character of his victim, with its weaknesses and possible failures under temptation, as well as its accomplished deflections from the paths of virtue, are laid bare in all their hideous nakedness before him."—*London Saturday Review.*

"Mr. Heron-Allen quotes learnedly from many writers in defence of his pet science . . . he claims for Cheirosophy the value almost of prophetic power, since the student may by its aid predict a blow by an observation of the tendencies which will bring about a misfortune."—*London Daily News.*

PUBLICATIONS OF G. P. PUTNAM'S SONS.

FOR GENERAL REFERENCE.

THE POCKET ATLAS OF THE WORLD. A comprehensive and popular series of 54 maps, illustrating political and physical geography. Prepared by JOHN BARTHOLOMEW, F.R.G.S. Beautifully printed in 32mo, cloth extra, $1 ; full leather $1 50

" A great marvel in a small compass."—*Chicago Advance.*

" A most inviting little tome, . . . legible and intelligible."—*N. Y. Commercial Advertiser.*

" One of the most convenient little books ever published. . . . It is a little marvel and full of compact information, and its maps are excellent."—*Chicago Tribune.*

" A decidedly 'cute pocket atlas."—*Cincinnati Commercial Gazette.*

" Its singularly tasteful and handy shape—a necessity to the traveller and all who 'live in trunks,' while exceedingly convenient to all."—*Congregationalist.*

" It is refreshing to find a thing so new, so unique, so correct, so serviceable. . . . It is all it purports to be, and is more and better than any one would suspect from the title or from any review that could be given it. It is what every student has wanted, what every office and home need. We would not be without it, personally, for several times its price."—*Boston Journal of Education.*

THE HAND-BOOK DICTIONARY. A practical and conversational dictionary of the English, French, and German languages in parallel columns. By GEORGE F. CHAMBERS, F.R.A. 18mo, roan, pp. xiii. + 724 . $2 00

" Altogether satisfactory."—*London Times.*

" An excellent hand-book for traveller or student."—*N. Y. Tribune.*

" Thoroughly well done. . . . Must prove very useful."—*Congregationalist.*

" It is literally a hand-book."—*N. Y. Critic.*

" To a tourist through France or Germany it is indispensable. It is the best work of the kind that has come into our hands."—*Indianapolis Journal.*

THE GLOBE PRONOUNCING GAZETTEER OF THE WORLD, DESCRIPTIVE AND STATISTICAL. Being a geographical dictionary for popular use. Octavo, cloth extra, with 32 maps . $2 50

" A gazetteer, like a dictionary, is never quite completed, but in these four hundred and sixty-two pages, in addition to the thirty-two maps, in double column of nonpareil type, an amount of information is gathered that is marvellous. We put the volume among our own choice books of reference."—*Churchman.*

G. P. PUTNAM'S SONS,

NEW YORK:
27 AND 29 WEST 23D ST.

LONDON:
27 KING WILLIAM ST., STRAND.

[OVER.